Sharing THE SUNDAY SCRIPTURES *with* *Youth*

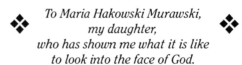

To Maria Hakowski Murawski,
my daughter,
who has shown me what it is like
to look into the face of God.

 Genuine recycled paper with 10% post-consumer waste.
Printed with soy-based ink.

The publishing team included Robert P. Stamschror, development editor; Laurie A. Berg, copy editor; Gary J. Boisvert, production editor and typesetter; Maurine R. Twait, art director; Stephan Nagel, cover designer; pre-press, printing, and binding by the graphics division of Saint Mary's Press.

The illustrations on pages 13, 23, 35, 51, and 75 in this book are from *Clip Art for Year C,* by Steve Erspamer (Chicago: Liturgy Training Publications, 1993). Copyright © 1993 by the Archdiocese of Chicago, 1800 North Hermitage Avenue, Chicago, IL 60622-1101. Used with permission. All rights reserved.

The acknowledgments continue on page 151.

Printed in the United States of America

Printing: 4

Year: 2003

ISBN 0-88489-431-2

Lectionary-Based Resources for Youth Ministry

Sharing THE SUNDAY SCRIPTURES *with* *Youth*

Cycle *C*

Maryann Hakowski

Saint Mary's Press
Winona, Minnesota
www.smp.org

Contents

Introduction

In the beginning was the Word, and the Word was with God, and the Word was God. (John 1:1, NRSV)

Recognizing the Hunger

Today's youth are hungry.
They are hungry for the word of God.
They are hungry for the Good News of Jesus Christ.
And many of them have not had a taste of it.

The Challenge of Catholic Youth Evangelization, by the National Federation for Catholic Youth Ministry, challenges youth ministers to feed the hungers of young people. The document identifies the following hungers:
- the hunger for meaning and purpose
- the hunger for connection
- the hunger for recognition
- the hunger for justice
- the hunger for the holy

(Pp. 5–6)

By effectively sharing the word of God with young people, we can help them find purpose and meaning for their lives. They will discover that they are connected with God and with others through a faith community in which God's word is shared, explored, and lived. They will find that God recognizes the gifts of all persons and celebrates their worth. They will see that God's word really is Good News for the oppressed, and it offers the possibility of countering the materialism and consumerism that are rampant in our world. Finally, they will find that God's purpose is to make them holy.

Overview

The Lectionary

The lectionary contains the Scripture readings for all the eucharistic celebrations (Sundays and weekdays) of the liturgical year. The liturgical year, and consequently the lectionary, begins with the first Sunday of Advent. It continues through the Christmas season, after which Ordinary Time begins. Ordinary Time is interrupted by the seasons of Lent and Easter, then it resumes and continues to the end of the liturgical year.

The Sunday readings are divided into three cycles that rotate year to year. The Gospel of Matthew is used in year A, the Gospel of Mark in year B, and the Gospel of Luke in year C. The Gospel of John has a special place in the Lenten and Easter seasons of all three cycles.

Each Sunday in the lectionary includes three readings and a psalm. The first reading is typically from the Hebrew Scriptures and is selected to relate with the Gospel reading. It often foreshadows something that will happen in the Gospel, and occasionally the Gospel even quotes it. The psalm usually complements the first reading and the Gospel. The second reading is from one of the letters of the Apostles. It is not chosen for its relationship with the other readings. Rather, it is intended to provide a semi-continuous reading of all the letters over the three-year period. The third reading is the Gospel, and it is taken from one of the four Gospels in the aforementioned fashion.

The resources in this book are based on the Scripture readings in the lectionary for the Sundays of the C cycle.

Why a Lectionary Approach?

Why choose the lectionary as the basis for a Scripture resource for teens? For many Catholics—including young people—exposure to the Bible comes primarily at Mass, when the Scriptures are read from the lectionary. For these Catholics, the activities in this book will review and reinforce the scriptural word they hear on Sunday. For those who do not attend Mass regularly, this book will put them in touch with the Sunday Scriptures and may even serve as an invitation to celebrate the Word with the community in the Sunday Eucharist.

Also, the Catholic lectionary offers an organized and thorough method for listening to God's word as it comes through the Scriptures. The selection of Sunday readings for the three cycles of the liturgical year ensures that the principal portions of God's word will be heard and considered over a suitable period of time.

At the same time, *Sharing the Sunday Scriptures with Youth: Cycle C* is not intended to be an alternative to the catechetical component of a youth ministry program, nor even as a substitute for the study of the Scriptures in a catechetical component. Rather, it is intended to be a Scripture-based supplement for ongoing catechesis and other elements of a youth ministry effort. This book can also serve as a connection between youth ministry efforts and Sunday liturgical celebrations in the parish.

The Activities

Action-Centered

The Scriptures are most often experienced by reading them or listening to them and then having them explained. The resources in this book go beyond that method. By way of hands-on activities, the participants not only hear and understand God's word but are actively engaged with it and are invited to respond in a personal way.

Relevant

The activities in *Sharing the Sunday Scriptures with Youth: Cycle C* make every attempt to be authentic both to the Scriptures and to the experiences of teens living in contemporary U.S. society. With the vast experiential differences among teens of different parts of the country in mind, as well as differences in age, race, and socioeconomic status, I chose activities that relate to needs, questions, concerns, and celebrations most common to all.

The scriptural themes on which the activities are based are chosen from the Sunday readings as a set rather than on a line or phrase from just one of the readings.

Diverse

This book employs a wide variety of activities and learning methods. The following list identifies each type of activity, along with a distinguishing icon. The icons will help you quickly locate a particular type of activity that you might want to use. Some activities are a combination of more than one type.

= affirmation = drama = journaling = Scripture study

= community service = family activity = music = storytelling

= craft = game that teaches = prayer = video resource

= discussion = icebreaker = reflection = witness talk

The Format   The resources for each Sunday are set up in the following sequence:

Initial Information

Each set of resources begins by identifying the Sunday of the year being considered, the lectionary reading number to help one find the readings for that Sunday in the lectionary, and the Scripture citations for that Sunday.

God's Word

The "God's Word" section contains a major theme drawn from the readings and a brief synopsis of the readings. Also included in this section are several additional themes called "Themes for Teens," which connect with the lived experience of today's teens.

Our Response

"Our Response" includes one specific, detailed activity with all the information you will need to prepare and facilitate it with a group of young people. This activity is usually based on the major theme that is drawn from the Scripture readings. Also included are several pithy activity ideas for alternative activities that are related to the suggested themes and connected with one or more of the Scripture readings.

Strategies and Contexts   The resources in this book can be used in many ways and in many settings. Select the way that appropriately addresses your setting and best engages your group of teens. Here are some possible uses:
- as starting points for weekly youth group meetings
- as Scripture-related supplements for youth group meetings
- as a general resource for planning retreats and lock-ins, or as quick ideas for meetings
- as aids for youth ministers who grapple with the Scriptures themselves, to ease their fears of using Scripture-related activities with young people
- as Scripture- and liturgy-related supplements for high school religion teachers, especially in courses on the Scriptures, the Mass, or the liturgical year
- as a homily help for pastors preparing for youth liturgies or any parish liturgy

Advantages   Using a lectionary-based resource with an activities approach has a number of advantages, including the following:

Excites Catholic youth about Scripture study. Most teens could think of at least ten things they would rather do than read the Bible. This book provides a variety of fun, exciting, and challenging ways of experiencing the Scriptures.

Engages youth with the Scriptures. The Bible is a whole library of books of different literary forms, so it can be intimidating at first glance. Most teens have no idea where to begin or even why they should open the Bible. The activities in this book give young people a taste of what is inside the Bible and an invitation to read more.

Promotes a lifelong habit of spending time with the Scriptures. Experiencing God's word in a more personal and meaningful way can encourage young people to make the Bible a lifelong companion.

Introduces the Scriptures as a tool for building relationships with God and others. The Scriptures include wonderful recipes for how to live in relationship with others and how to relate to God. Teens are always struggling with relationships. They are often pulling away from parents and moving toward peers. This resource pays special attention to relationships with one's self, others, and God.

Encourages adults who work with youth to spend more time with the Scriptures. Many adults working with youth—especially volunteers—are intimidated by anything related to the Scriptures or prayer. A synopsis of the Scripture readings for each Sunday is provided to familiarize such persons with the readings and to help them use the learning activities to open the Word with young people.

Makes spending time with the Scriptures exciting and meaningful. Approaching the Scriptures with a sense of adventure invites teens to unlock the mysteries found there. With some guidance and creative ways for unlocking these mysteries, teens will be encouraged to delve into them to find meaning for themselves.

Explores symbols and rituals found in the Scriptures. Taking part in the activities in this book, especially the prayer experiences, allows young people to experience the rich symbolism in the passages they read. They will discover, firsthand, connections between Catholic rituals and rituals portrayed in the Scriptures.

Helps young people experience the Scriptures as good news in a world filled with bad news. Young people today are in great need of hope. They see many reasons for despair as they look around at their families, their communities, and their world. The Scriptures can help them discover and celebrate the goodness in themselves and others as well as the good news of salvation through Jesus Christ.

Begins with the Bible message. Many youth Bible programs begin with critical issues facing youth and try to weave the Bible in where they can. This resource is different in that it *begins* with the Scriptures and relates its message to developmental, relational, and societal issues in the lives of teens.

Enables teens to make connections between the Scriptures and their own life. The Scriptures come alive when they find expression in life. The activities in this book engage teens and help them actively apply the Scriptures to their own experience.

Proclaims the Good News effectively and enables young people to proclaim the Good News in return. Sharing the Scriptures with young people is only the beginning of evangelization. Jesus preached the Word to his disciples, related it to their lives, and taught them how to share it. This resource helps young people find the language and the courage to share the Good News with others.

Limitations
Using a lectionary-based approach to exploring the Scriptures with youth has some limitations. First, a strict lectionary-based approach—one that always uses the resources for the current Sunday—may not match the needs and circumstances of a particular group of young people at a particular time. It may be necessary to look to another Sunday's readings—or even a Scripture passage not in the lectionary—for a theme and activities that speak to a current happening.

Second, the Scripture readings chosen for the three cycles of the Catholic lectionary do not encompass all the readings in the Bible. Studying only the Scriptures included in the lectionary ignores a number of books of the Bible, especially some of those in the Hebrew Scriptures.

Finally, the resources found here are by no means designed to replace the liturgy of the word at Mass. And though it may be true, unfortunately, that many teens do not attend liturgy on Sunday, this sharing of the Scriptures should be a means of inviting them back to Mass rather than a replacement or excuse for missing Mass.

The Challenge
In her book *Fashion Me a People,* Maria Harris suggests that the key to Scripture study is knowing the Word, interpreting the Word, living the Word, and doing the Word (pp. 60–61).

Our challenge is to enable young people to experience the Word, grapple with its meaning, connect it to their own life, share it with their peers, and find the courage to respond to the God revealed in it.

Being a minister of the Word to young people is challenging, but it is eye opening and exciting, too. One cannot help but be changed in experiencing the Scriptures through the eyes of a young person.

One of my favorite Scripture passages is the one in which Jesus feeds the hungry with both the word of God and bread and fish, blessed and shared.

We need the word of God, blessed and shared, to fill our hunger. May God bless you in your ministry and nourish you and your young people as you share the word of God together.

And the Word became flesh and lived among us. (John 1:14, NRSV)

Advent

First Sunday of Advent

Scripture Readings
(3)

- ❖ Jer. 33:14–16
- ❖ Ps. 25:4–5,8–9,10,14
- ❖ 1 Thess. 3:12—4:2
- ❖ Luke 21:25–28,34–36

God's Word

A major theme of the Scripture readings is "Waiting for Christ to return."

Both the first reading and the Gospel talk about the coming of the Messiah, a promise found in Jeremiah and echoed by other prophets in the Hebrew Scriptures. The Messiah will come from the line of David and rule with justice. The first reading talks about a promise that Christians believe is fulfilled in the coming of Christ.

The psalmist trusts in God so completely that he lifts up not only his hands and heart but his whole being. The act of lifting up reflects openness. The psalmist sees God as teacher and guide and asks to walk and talk with God.

The writer of the First Letter to the Thessalonians wanted to keep the Thessalonians from being discouraged when the Second Coming of Christ did not happen quickly, according to their schedule. Paul tells them that the best way to wait for the Lord's return is to grow in love for God and for one another. Their love for one another ought to be as great as Paul's love for them. Paul prays that God will strengthen their hearts to live holy and blameless lives, so that when Christ does return, they can rejoice with him.

All of today's readings are caught between promise and fulfillment. The Gospel reading is full of anticipation and expectation, but we learn that the return of the Messiah may not be quite what we expect. The Gospel of Luke paints a frightening scene of strange signs in the sun and moon and of people scared to death. Instead of becoming "bloated with indulgence and . . . worldly cares," we are invited to pray and to be prepared for the coming of the Son of God. Setting aside earthly cares is especially hard at this time of the year, when it is easy to get caught up in the commercialism of the season. The Gospel suggests that each day of our life is to be lived as if Jesus might arrive any minute.

Themes for Teens

The following themes from the Scriptures relate to the lives of teens:
- God keeps promises.
- We wait for Jesus.
- Learn how to wait.
- Lift yourself up to God.
- Grow in love.

Our Response

Activity

Are You Open to Advent?

This activity is keyed to the readings as a whole. The following story invites the young people to reflect on their attitude as they enter the season of Advent. It asks them to be open to the spiritual gifts of the season and to prepare their heart for the coming of Jesus.

For this reflection it is ideal to have three bowls, one upside down; one upright, but cracked and filled with dirt; and a third, upright, clean, and empty. You may want to pour water into each bowl as you read the story. Do not tell the teens that the water represents themselves. Allow them to draw their own connections from the story.

The Story of Three Bowls

The first bowl is upside down; nothing can go into it. When someone tries to pour something into this bowl, the liquid runs off. The second bowl is upright, but it has many cracks and contains some debris. Anything poured into this bowl becomes polluted or leaks through the cracks. The third bowl is clean and without cracks or holes.

The bowls can represent our attitude as we begin the season of Advent. Are we like the first bowl—close-minded, unable or unwilling to hear the Good News about the coming of Christ? Are we like the second bowl—filled with our own prejudices and experiences and, therefore, not able to take in what is being offered? Or, are we like the third bowl—open and ready to receive Jesus into our heart and mind this Advent season? (Adapted from Gargiulo, "God Gives Us Fresh Clay," p. 19)

Activity Ideas

The following activity ideas also relate to the Scripture readings. You may want to read the passage(s) indicated as part of the activity.

- In today's psalm we pray: "Your ways, O Lord, make known to me; / teach me your paths, / guide me in your truth and teach me."
  - If God showed up one day at your school, what subject would God teach? Why?
  - How do you think God would teach?
  - What would your classroom be like?
  - Do you think your classmates would treat God the way they treat other teachers?
  - How would class be different?

  Divide into small groups and create short skits entitled "A Most Unusual Substitute Teacher." Share the skits with the entire group. Discuss what we can learn from Jesus, our teacher. (Ps. 25:4–5,8–9,10,14)

- Before your meeting starts, direct everyone into a room other than your regular meeting room. The room should be empty except for a few chairs and a large sign that says "Waiting Room." Leave the teens in the room for 10 minutes without any instruction. Later, when you are all together, ask how they felt about having to wait. What did they do with the time while they were waiting? Finally, ask, "What are you going to do while waiting for Jesus?" Give each teen a small, bumper-sticker-size sign that says "Waiting Room," and ask them to hang it in their room during Advent as a reminder to make good use of their time before the coming of Jesus at Christmas. (All readings)

- Give each young person a noisemaker like those used at New Year's Eve celebrations. At your signal, invite them to yell "Happy New Year," making as much noise as they can. Explain to the young people that the first week of the new year, according to the liturgical year of the church, is this week. Show them a copy of a liturgical calendar and compare it with a regular calendar. Explain the seasons of the church year and how we as Catholics prepare for the coming of Christmas during the season of Advent. (All readings)

- If your class or youth group meets weekly in the same place, consider setting up a crèche and adding a piece to it each week for the next eight weeks, through the Advent and Christmas seasons. This week place a figure in the crèche with a small sign on it that says "me," and emphasize the need for the teens to place themselves in the Christmas story so that they can experience it on a deeper level this year. Let the young people decide, based on the readings each week, which figure to add to the scene. (All readings)

Second Sunday of Advent

**Scripture Readings
(6)**

❖ Bar. 5:1–9
❖ Ps. 126:1–2,2–3,4–5,6
❖ Phil. 1:4–6,8–11
❖ Luke 3:1–6

God's Word

A major theme of the Scripture readings is "A call to change."

The first reading is full of joy and triumph. Jerusalem is told to take off the dark clothes of mourning and to put on the splendor of God. Baruch recounts the return of the exiles to Jerusalem and their celebration. The promise is fulfilled. The prophet tells everyone to stand in the highest place and see all that God has done, the good all around them. We do not need to climb the closest mountain, but we need to live our life with our eyes open so that we can see God's glory all around us.

Have you ever taken God for granted? The psalmist hasn't. The Lord *has* done great things for us. Do we respond with joy? This psalm reflects the triumphant homecoming described in the first reading. The psalmist celebrates what God has already done and looks forward to future blessings.

In this letter written in captivity, Paul thanks the Philippians for their support, and urges them to grow in love and to be ready for Christ when he comes. Prison has not dampened the writer's enthusiasm for Christ, and he urges the Philippians to keep up the good work they have started as they wait for the return of Jesus Christ. We, too, are urged to value what really matters in our life, to sift out the unimportant from the important. It is not the wrapping paper or the tinsel, the Christmas TV specials or the holiday sales, or the cookies and Santa Claus that really matter. What we hold in our heart—our love for God and family and friends—is what really matters.

The Gospel reading echoes the words of the prophet Isaiah and sets the stage for the ministry of John the Baptist. Last week the psalmist asked us to walk in God's path. Today the Gospel writer describes John the Baptist as clearing a straight path for God. John is a bridge between the prophets of the Hebrew Scriptures and the coming of Jesus. This reading gives us a sense of history by naming the political leaders of the day, and it points to the dramatic change that will occur in the world with the coming of Christ. In order to prepare for his coming, we are called simply to recognize our sins, repent, and be forgiven. In a holiday filled with receiving, the Gospel reading asks us to repent, to prepare, and to hope, so that we may be a light to all peoples.

Themes for Teens

The following themes from the Scriptures relate to the lives of teens:
- Walk the walk of God.
- Change your life.
- Be open to change.
- Hear the voice in the desert.
- Keep up the good work.

Our Response

Activity **Change Your Life**

This icebreaker is keyed to the Gospel reading. It is designed to get the young people thinking about ways they can make changes in their own life. They are urged to answer the call of John the Baptist to repent, to prepare, and to hope.

Have the teens each bring a one-dollar bill to the meeting. Ask them how they can make change for their dollar. If they cannot make their own change or get change from someone else, allow them to make change with coins you provide.

Read the Gospel reading together. Invite the young people to make the connection between the icebreaker activity and the reading.

For each quarter, ask them to think of one way that they can repent this Advent. For each dime, ask them to think of one way that they can be more hopeful this Advent. For each nickel or penny, ask them to think of one way that they can better prepare for Jesus' coming at the end of Advent.

Remind them that we can work for change ourselves, seek the help of others in our efforts to change, and call on God to help us change.

Encourage the teens to keep the coins in their pocket or purse through Advent as a reminder of John the Baptist and his call to change.

Activity Ideas The following activity ideas also relate to the Scripture readings. You may want to read the passage(s) indicated as part of the activity.

- John calls us into the desert and urges us to make the time to pray. Ask the young people to brainstorm some ways to bring prayer home to their family during Advent. Urge them to be creative and to think of ways to involve every member of their family—such as incorporating crafts with prayers for children, creating a prayer book to send to Grandma, or lighting a candle on the Advent wreath. Compile a booklet or a list of the teens' ideas and send one home to each family. Encourage the teens to have family prayer time every day, or at least twice a week, during the rest of Advent. (Luke 3:1–6)

- This week's readings urge us to praise God for deliverance, to take joy in the great things God has done for us, to grow in love, and to make straight the path. This season of the year is filled with so many distractions that it is often hard to find God. Ask the teens to answer the following questions in their journal: What if the Son of God arrives and no one even notices? What are you going to do to tune out some of the distractions of the season and tune in Jesus? (All readings)

- After reading today's Gospel, ask, What is the real reason for this season? Give the teens a variety of craft supplies and ask them to make Advent cards instead of Christmas cards to send to friends and family members. The wording on the cards should say, "Jesus is the reason for the season." Avoid using commercial symbols of the season; instead, cut out nativity scenes from last year's Christmas cards and use them to decorate the Advent cards. (Luke 3:1–6)

- Ask the teens to make a list of things they need to do or buy before Christmas Day arrives. Tape all the lists together to make one long list. Next, ask the teens to help John the Baptist make an Advent list. What would be on John's list? Start with ideas gleaned from today's Scripture readings. (All readings)

Third Sunday of Advent

Scripture Readings (9)
- ❖ Zeph. 3:14–18
- ❖ Isa. 12:2–3,4,5–6
- ❖ Phil. 4:4–7
- ❖ Luke 3:10–18

God's Word

A major theme of the Scripture readings is "Rejoice! Jesus is coming!"

The first reading from Zephaniah is the song of celebration and rejoicing of a people who have found salvation. They rejoice for two reasons—the bad times are behind them, and God has returned to dwell with them. God even joins them in song. Zephaniah, who is often called the prophet of doom, in this case paints a comforting image of God. We, too, celebrate the discovery of God in our midst.

The responsorial psalm does not convey mere happiness, but is a cry of joy and gladness. This responsorial is not drawn from the Book of Psalms but from Isaiah, who is often called the prophet of Advent. Isaiah brings the good news of salvation, and he witnesses to the coming of the Messiah. This psalm urges us to give thanks and praise to God and is also an expression of confidence that God is always there for us.

The second reading, too, is full of rejoicing. We are told that life is too short to worry about everything. We are urged to rid ourselves of anxiety—often a tough thing to do—and to take all our needs to God.

The people ask John the Baptist what they should be doing while waiting for the Messiah. Not all of them are sincere about repentance. John demands that they show their sincerity in action. He tells them to think about the have-nots, especially those in need of the basics, such as food and clothing. He tells them to stop bullying others and to be fair in their financial dealings. Because of John's words, some want to know if John is the Messiah. John sets them straight right away and uses the symbol of tying Jesus' sandal straps to show that he is the servant of the Lord.

John promises that baptism with water is only the first step and that Jesus will baptize us with the fire of the Holy Spirit. For John, the best way to prepare for the coming of Jesus is to preach the Good News and to live a good life. For us, it takes courage to ask, "What should we do as we wait?"

Themes for Teens

The following themes from the Scriptures relate to the lives of teens:
- Start the celebration.
- Jesus is coming!
- Get ready for Jesus.
- Don't waste your waiting time.
- Be fair to others.

Our Response

Activity

Sharing the Joy of Jesus

This craft activity is keyed to the readings as a whole. It gives the teens an opportunity to share the joy of Jesus by making ornaments they can give to others, for example, to residents of a nursing home or a homeless shelter.

You will need green poster board, red and white curling ribbon, miniature candy canes, scissors, glue, red markers, and a hole punch for this craft.

Trace a heart approximately 6 inches high and 6 inches wide onto green poster board. Cut out the heart and punch a hole at the top. Loop a white piece of curling ribbon through the hole as a hanger. Tie the red pieces through the hole also, but instead of tying the ends together, curl them with a scissors for decoration. Glue an upside down candy cane to one side of the heart to represent the letter *J*. Add the letters *oy* with the marker to complete the word *Joy*. Glue another upside down candy cane to the other side of the heart as another *J*. This time add the letters *esus* to spell *Jesus*.

Encourage the young people to deliver the ornaments in person so they can experience the "joy" of giving.

Activity Ideas

The following activity ideas also relate to the Scripture readings. You may want to read the passage(s) indicated as part of the activity.

- In the Gospel we read a little about two sacraments of initiation. Ask the teens to identify the sacraments and to answer the following questions:
  - Which sacrament is missing from this reading?
  - How are the symbols of fire and water important in this reading and in these sacraments?
  - How does each sacrament bring us closer to God?

  Close by praying—by name if possible—for the infants to be baptized soon in your community, for the children preparing for first communion, and for the teens preparing for confirmation. (Luke 3:10–18)

- Today's excerpt from the Letter to the Philippians promises "God's own peace, which is beyond all understanding." Tack a map of the world to a large bulletin board. Give each teen a pin with praying hands on it, or glue small pictures of praying hands onto thumbtacks. Ask the teens to offer a prayer for a country in need of peace and to place their pin on that spot. The teens could offer all the prayers today, or make the prayers part of an on-going prayer throughout the year. (Phil. 4:4–7)

- All the readings today tell us that God is near. Invite the teens to search for a story or a video about a conversion in which a person experiences God through other people. It can be a fictional story, a real-life witness, a video movie, or a TV episode. Then discuss the question, "How do we experience the closeness of God through others?" The weeks before Christmas, in particular, are filled with stories about people touched by God. (All readings)

- John tells the tax collectors to be good tax collectors and the soldiers to be better soldiers. Instead of encouraging the young people to do more things or new things this Advent, direct them to think of ways they can be better Christians in the life they are living right now. In their journal, ask the teens to reflect on ways they can be better students, better daughters or sons, better employees, or better friends. (Luke 3:10–18)

Fourth Sunday of Advent

Scripture Readings
(12)
- ❖ Mic. 5:1–4
- ❖ Ps. 80:2–3,15–16,18–19
- ❖ Heb. 10:5–10
- ❖ Luke 1:39–45

God's Word

A major theme of the Scripture readings is "Say yes to God!"

Micah is one of the prophets who point to the coming of the Messiah. He tells the people of Israel that their suffering will come to an end when a shepherd-king is born to the tribe of Judah in Bethlehem. This shepherd-king will have humble roots, but he is the one who was promised a long time ago, in the days of King David. Just as we will later hear in the Christian Testament, Jesus is called shepherd and bringer of peace. Into a world filled with violence comes hope and peace. Jesus will come as a shepherd for all people.

"Lord, make us turn to you, let us see your face and we shall be saved." It is hard to turn away from all the distractions of the Christmas season, especially this last week as it reaches a fever pitch. How do we turn away from the image of Santa Claus and turn toward the face of Jesus? The psalmist tells us that we do not have to do it alone. God is our help. Let us pray that God will help us turn toward the real meaning of Christmas.

The second reading is a stark reminder of the connection between Advent and Lent, between Christmas and Easter. Jesus is coming to do the will of the Father, and God's will allows that Jesus will die for our sins. By being obedient to the will of the Father during his life, even though doing so brought about his death, Jesus saves us. The coming of Jesus is not an accident. Jesus' birth at Christmas is the beginning of the fulfillment of God's plan for our salvation.

In the Gospel, we follow Mary on a quick journey to visit her cousin Elizabeth. Both women are unexpectedly expecting: Elizabeth—older and without a child for so long; Mary—young, unmarried, and hearing the news from an angel. Mary was concerned for Elizabeth, but it is Elizabeth who is filled with joy and prayer at the sight of Mary. Her words are part of the Hail Mary that we pray as Catholic Christians: "'Blessed are you among women and blessed is the fruit of your womb.'" Mary recognizes the presence of God and responds in prayer. This prayer is called the Magnificat. Even John the Baptist responds to Jesus by stirring in the womb of his mother, Elizabeth.

Themes for Teens

The following themes from the Scriptures relate to the lives of teens:
- The Prince of Peace is coming.
- Be open to God's will.
- Without Christmas, there is no Easter.
- Your will be done.
- Blessed are you, Mary.

Our Response

Activity

Unexpectedly Expecting

This outreach project is keyed to the readings as a whole. It is something different from the traditional projects of caroling at a nursing home or filling Christmas baskets for the poor at this time of the year.

Contact a local pregnancy crisis center or an agency that helps unwed or homeless new mothers. Ask for a list of needs for newborns. As a youth group or class, collect items for a Christmas present for at least one expectant mother. You may want to target a pregnant teen as a way for the young people to reach out to other teens. Items might include diapers, wipes, bottles, baby clothes, baby food, or blankets. If you want the young people to plan a bigger project, get the parish involved and provide for several moms-to-be who are in need. You may want to include a prayer for the new mother and child with the gifts.

Activity Ideas

The following activity ideas also relate to the Scripture readings. You may want to read the passage(s) indicated as part of the activity.

- Note that in the Gospel reading, Elizabeth recognizes the presence of God in Mary. Then pose these questions for journal reflection:
  - Do others recognize the presence of God in you?
  - Do you recognize the presence of God in yourself?

  (Luke 1:39–45)

- Ask each teen to bring in his or her own rosary or a family rosary. If some teens do not have one, purchase some inexpensive ones to share. Review with, or in some cases teach, the teens how to pray the rosary. Pray one decade together and ask the teens to finish praying the rest of the rosary between now and Christmas Day. (Luke 1:39–45)

- List some of the many ways Jesus is described in the first reading. Send the teens to the Scriptures to find other names. Tell each teen to choose a different name and to make an ornament to illustrate the name. The teens can use a symbol—such as a shepherd's staff for "Shepherd"—or they can do a stylized design of a name, such as "Emmanuel." Instead of the traditional Jesse tree, decorate a Jesus tree with the ornaments made by the young people and place it in a common area for all the members of your school or parish community to enjoy. (Mic. 5:1–4)

- As a quiet reflection at the end of your meeting, play the song "Mary, Did You Know?" It has been recorded by several artists, including Michael English on *Michael English,* Mark Lowery on *Remotely Controlled,* and Kenny Rogers on *The Gift.* (Luke 1:39–45)

Christmas

Sunday in the Octave of Christmas (Holy Family)

Scripture Readings (17)

❖ Sir. 3:2–6,12–14
❖ Ps. 128:1–2,3,4–5
❖ Col. 3:12–21
❖ Luke 2:41–52

God's Word

A major theme of the Scripture readings is "Love God and family."

The reading from Sirach expands on the commandment to honor one's mother and father. Although the word *respect* is not used directly, *honor, reverence, comfort, kindness,* and *consideration* all add up to respect. The reading informs us that God holds parents in a special place of honor. Treating parents the way God prescribes will lead to riches, children, a long life, atonement, and many other good things. Obedience to parents is equated with obedience to God.

The psalm seems directed at the head of the family, suggesting that if the head of the family fears the Lord and walks in the ways of God, good things will come to the family. Fear of the Lord does not mean that God is unapproachable or that we should be frightened of God. It means that we should treat God with reverence and respect as our Creator and Savior.

The passage from Colossians, in effect, is the blueprint for living as a Christian family. It gives specific instructions for how Christians and Christian families are to act toward one another and toward God. In general, the passage calls us to put on the love of Christ and allow that love to guide all our actions.

Rare in the Gospels are stories about Jesus' daily life as a child growing up with his parents. We assume that he played like other children play and that he suffered the usual growing pains that come with adolescence. Here we see Jesus going with his parents on the annual trip to Jerusalem to celebrate Passover. But Jesus does not leave with them; he stays behind. When Mary and Joseph discover him missing, they return to Jerusalem and find the boy preaching and teaching in the Temple.

Jesus' parents are upset and do not understand when Jesus says, "'Did you not know I had to be in my Father's house?'" However, we learn that Jesus, though he was taken up with God and things of the Temple, went home and remained obedient to his parents as he learned and grew.

This is more than a story about a missing child and frantic parents. Jesus announces his relationship with God the Father and says that he will eventually loosen family ties to follow the Father's will.

Themes for Teens

The following themes from the Scriptures relate to the lives of teens:
- Respect your parents.
- Walk in God's ways.
- Put on love.
- God's house is our home.
- Jesus wows the Temple.

Our Response

Activity **A Family Prayer for Christmas**

This take-home activity is keyed to all the readings. It encourages the young people to pray with their family. It invites families to discover the family blessings in Christmas and to focus on the real meaning of the season.

Since most youth groups and schools do not meet between Christmas and New Year's, you may want to send this prayer home with the young people and encourage them to share it with their family at a holiday meal.

A Family Prayer for Christmas

O
Jesus,
our Savior,
thank you for
living among us
and showing us the
way to God. Thank you
for being born at Christmas.
Your presence among us is our
greatest gift. Thank you, too, for
all the virtues you give us as we try
to follow you. Thank you for faith, hope,
charity, peace, thanksgiving, joy, patience,
contentment, kindness, generosity, moderation,
listening, honesty, gentleness, silence, self-control,
forgiveness, obedience, respect, humility, faithfulness,
compassion, cheerfulness, enthusiasm, and for all the gifts
and talents you have so generously given to our family.
Thank you
especially for
one another.
Bless and watch over our family
on this Christmas Day and always. Amen.

(Costello, *Advent Prayers for Families,* n.p.)

Activity Ideas The following activity ideas also relate to the Scripture readings. You may want to read the passage(s) indicated as part of the activity.

- Jesus, even as a young boy, felt a need to be in his Father's house. Ask the young people:
  - Where is "God's house" for you?
  - Do you attend Mass as a family, or does each person in your family go to a different Mass?

  Make an early New Year's resolution to spend more time as a family—at parish or other functions. What are some recreational, service, educational, or spiritual things you can do as a family? (All readings)

- Direct the teens to write their own version of the Twelve Days of Christmas. For each day, ask them to think of one thing they can do for a family member, for example, doing the dishes without complaining, letting their brother borrow their new rollerblades, taking out the trash for their dad, baby-sitting a younger sibling so their parents can go out on a "date." (All readings)

- By now everyone in your family has opened their presents. Perhaps you got a sweater for Mom, a tie for Dad, and a CD for your sister. What about giving some presents that last longer? Ask the teens to think about one talent or gift or good quality they appreciate in a family member. Have them write that quality on a small piece of paper, put it inside a small box, and wrap it with leftover scraps of Christmas paper. Tell them to hide the tiny presents inside the branches of the Christmas tree, and send the family members searching for their affirmation boxes. Remind the teens to let their family know how much they care after the holidays are over, too. (All readings)

Second Sunday After Christmas

Scripture Readings (19)

❖ Sir. 24:1–4,8–12
❖ Ps. 147:12–13,14–15,19–20
❖ Eph. 1:3–6,15–18
❖ John 1:1–18

God's Word

A major theme of the Scripture readings is "The Word became flesh."

The reading from Sirach gives wisdom a voice. Wisdom says that she comes from the mouth of God and has been given a special place in the heavens to dwell. She does not remain in the heavens, but comes down to dwell in the people as the word of God.

The psalm celebrates the word of God sent to live among us. The word of God is not an abstract concept; it is the intimate presence of God that is part of the fabric of human life. The psalm points toward the great mystery of Jesus coming as the incarnate Word of God.

The second reading shows that Jesus, the incarnate Word of God, is the center of God's plan for our salvation. The Letter to the Ephesians talks about how God sent Jesus to bring blessings firsthand and that in union with Jesus, people become adopted children of God. The author celebrates the Ephesian community's faith in Jesus. He prays for the gift of wisdom so that they will learn more about God, through Jesus, and grow closer to God.

The Gospel reading from John is the definitive statement about Jesus as the Word of God made flesh. We learn that the word of God was present in the beginning with the Creator, and, in time, became flesh in Jesus, the life and light for all. Jesus is the real light that came into the world and is a gift meant to be shared by all.

Themes for Teens

The following themes from the Scriptures relate to the lives of teens:
• Jesus is the Word of God.
• God grant us wisdom.
• The Word is God.
• Jesus is the Light of the World.
• The Word became flesh.

Our Response

Activity

Search for Wisdom

This activity is keyed to the first and second readings. It encourages the young people to search for words of wisdom in the Scriptures and in the traditions of other countries, and to start collecting reflections in their own book of wisdom.

Write each of the following proverbs on a small card and hide the cards around your meeting area before the teens arrive.

- Don't see all you see, and don't hear all you hear. (Irish proverb)
- In doing we learn. (English proverb)
- For the benefit of the flowers, we water the thorns. (Egyptian proverb)
- Be not afraid of growing slowly; be afraid only of standing still. (Chinese proverb)
- A person with a sour face should not open shop. (Latin proverb)
- The rower reaches the shore, partly by pulling, partly by letting go. (Egyptian proverb)
- The best speaker is the one who can turn the ear into an eye. (Arabian proverb)
- A good example is like a bell that calls many to church. (Danish proverb)
- God gives every bird its worm, but God does not throw it into the nest. (Swedish proverb)
- A good laugh and a long sleep are the two best cures. (Irish proverb)
- With God, go over the sea. Without God, don't even go over the threshold. (Russian proverb)

(Svoboda, "Beginning-of-the-Year Wisdom," p. 13)

Give each teen a medium-size notebook. On your signal, tell the teens to search around the meeting area for wisdom and to write what they find in their own book. When they finish, divide them into groups of four. Give each group a Bible, and ask the groups to search for and record short examples of words of wisdom. Direct them to find at least two examples from the Hebrew Scriptures and two from the Christian Testament.

Encourage the teens to take their book home and keep adding words of wisdom, both secular and biblical. If the teens in your group already keep a regular journal, you could ask them to leave a space at the bottom of each page or in a special section in the back for words of wisdom.

Activity Ideas

The following activity ideas also relate to the Scripture readings. You may want to read the passage(s) indicated as part of the activity.

- Pass a Bible around the circle and ask each young person to share one thing that she or he has learned from the word of God. Then pass a flashlight around the circle and ask each teen to share one way that God is the light of her or his life. (Ps. 147:12–13,14–15,19–20; Eph. 1:3–6,15–18; John 1:1–18)

- Give each teen a plastic electric candle. Introduce the reflection in the following way:
  - At this time of the year, many people are taking down their Christmas lights. We can't pack away our celebration of the true Light of the World along with the Christmas decorations.

    Ask the young people to light the candle in their window at home every night when they go to bed, as a reminder and a celebration that the Light of Christ has come into the world. (John 1:1–18)

- Divide the teens into four groups. Give each group one of the four readings for today. Ask each group to read its passage together and answer the following questions:
  - How does God's word speak to you?
  - How can this word become flesh? (How can you make it come alive in your life?)

Bring the four groups together and share their responses in a large group. (All readings)

- The reading from the Letter to the Ephesians is a beautiful blessing. Pray the prayer as if it were written directly for you, replacing each "us" with "me" and each "our" with "my." (Eph. 1:3–6,15–18)

Epiphany Sunday

Scripture Readings (20)

- ❖ Isa. 60:1–6
- ❖ Ps. 72:1–2,7–8,10–11,12–13
- ❖ Eph. 3:2–3,5–6
- ❖ Matt. 2:1–12

God's Word

A major theme of the Scripture readings is "Jesus comes for all."

The first reading, like last week's readings, foreshadows the coming of Jesus as the Light of the World. The author uses imagery of the rising and setting sun to portray God's favor and disfavor. Light is used to show when God is happy, or glad. Darkness usually means the people are in trouble. We are told to raise our head, open our eyes, and see how different the world looks when lit by the radiance of God.

The psalm echoes the last part of the first reading—that God is God for many nations, not just the people of Israel. Today, the birth of Jesus is celebrated all over the world by people of different races, ages, and economic means. The psalm reads as a tribute to a king—a king who is just and who has a place for afflicted people in the Kingdom.

The passage from the Letter to the Ephesians, like the first reading and the psalm, states that the Gospel is not meant for just one select group of people, but is to be shared with all. The secret (mystery) that the author talks about is, in fact, that the Kingdom of God is for everyone. The Gospel is not to be kept quiet. We must proclaim it from the rooftops.

Matthew's Gospel passage relates the story of the astrologers (often referred to as Kings, Wise Men, or Magi) who follow a star to find the newborn Jesus, who they heard was the Messiah. These kings are not Jews, but they come with gifts to pay homage to Jesus, who was born for all, not just for one group. The kings are not only on a physical journey, they are on a spiritual journey as well. They do not really know where they are going, but they just keep following the star and trusting that God will get them there. Like the kings, we are also on a spiritual journey, and we can trust that God will show us the way to Jesus.

Themes for Teens

The following themes from the Scriptures relate to the lives of teens:
- Walk in the light.
- In God's eyes, we are all equal.
- We are one in Christ.
- We are to proclaim the Gospel, not keep it quiet.
- Honor Jesus with your gifts.

Our Response

Activity   **The Reason for the Season**

This reflection activity is keyed to the readings as a whole. The Magi had to follow a star far from home to discover the real meaning of Christmas. This reflection asks the young people to keep Christ in Christmas all year long.

    Give each teen a copy of the drawing below. As the holiday season draws to an end, ask the young people to reflect quietly on how well they did at keeping Christ in Christmas and how they can keep the true spirit of Christmas alive all year long.

Activity Ideas   The following activity ideas also relate to the Scripture readings. You may want to read the passage(s) indicated as part of the activity.

- Ask someone who knows about astronomy to take the young people outside at night and help them identify the stars in the early January sky. Find the North Star, sometimes believed to be the Star of Bethlehem talked about it in today's Gospel. Ask:
  ○ How did the star point the way for the wise men to find Jesus?
  ○ Who are some of the stars in our life that point us to Jesus?

(Matt. 2:1–12)

- After sharing today's readings, take the teens outside at the end of the meeting to pray this rhyme, followed by quiet reflection.

  Star light, star bright,
  First star I see tonight.
  I wish I may. I wish I might.
  Pray this prayer I pray tonight.

(Matt. 2:1–12)

- Purchase some glow-in-the-dark star stickers. After sharing today's readings, give the teens each a star sticker to put on the ceiling of their room at home. Every night when they go to bed, they can remember to say a short prayer asking God to help them follow the star to Jesus. If you cannot locate stickers, you may want to use paint. Put a small amount of paint in several baby food jars for the teens to take home. Remind them to ask their parents before painting stars on their ceiling. (Matt. 2:1–12)

- In today's psalm we pray, "Lord, every nation on earth will adore you." If your group is able to gather for a last celebration of the Christmas season, ask each young person to bring a traditional ethnic Christmas food to share. After the meal, talk about other traditions from around the world that help us celebrate the true meaning of Christmas. (Ps. 72:1–2,7–8,10–11,12–13)

Baptism of the Lord Sunday

Scripture Readings (21)
- ❖ Isa. 42:1–4,6–7
- ❖ Ps. 29:1–2,3–4,3,9–10
- ❖ Acts 10:34–38
- ❖ Luke 3:15–16,21–22

God's Word

A major theme of the Scripture readings is "Born to serve the world."

The reading from Isaiah carries a promise that God will send a servant to establish justice on the earth. The Servant Savior is quiet and gentle, does not make much noise, but is also powerful, bringing justice to the entire world. This reading foreshadows Jesus—a servant empowered by God to bring justice, a light for all nations who will open the eyes of the blind and save those who are imprisoned by injustice.

The psalm bears a blessing of peace. Unlike the quiet servant in the first reading, here God's voice thunders over all the waters. We are called to praise and honor this mighty God. Our reward for our reverence will be a blessing of peace.

The reading from Acts makes it clear that the Good News about Jesus is for all people to hear, that Jesus Christ is the Lord of all, and that the goodness of peace is God's desire and gift for all.

The passage from Luke's Gospel tells of Jesus' baptism by John. Jesus' baptism marks the beginning of his mission to preach about repentance and the arrival of God's Kingdom. The imagery and God's words confirm that Jesus is truly the servant God has promised to send into the world to bring justice and peace to all. John's work of preparing the way is now done. The one who follows him, and who is more powerful than he, is now present.

Themes for Teens

The following themes from the Scriptures relate to the lives of teens:
- Jesus is a light to all nations.
- The Good News does not discriminate.
- God keeps promises.
- Jesus is God's Son.
- Baptism calls us to serve.

Our Response

Baptism Word Search

This word-search activity is keyed to the Gospel reading. It invites the young people to identify some of the key concepts and symbols related to the sacrament of baptism.

Give each teen a copy of the word search below. Ask the teens to find twelve words or phrases relating to the sacrament of baptism. Direct them to take turns identifying a word they found and explaining how it relates to the sacrament.

If you have extra time, invite the teens to find sixteen additional words or phrases, four from each of the readings today.

```
H   S   W   E   N   D   O   O   G   I   N   K   C   I   P   J
E   O   O   F   M   G   N   L   I   O   I   L   C'  E   D   H
C   A   R   X   M   E   S   S   I   A   H   R   A   B   J   O
U   W   T   I   Z   X   T   T   W   C   V   C   T   O   R   L
Q   E   P   S   G   O   A   N   R   O   E   N   H   T   E   Y
J   L   T   L   M   I   N   K   E   M   E   N   O   H   T   S
E   C   N   E   T   H   N   I   F   M   G   D   L   G   A   P
C   O   A   I   V   C   E   A   R   U   A   E   I   I   W   I
I   M   N   B   I   Z   A   L   N   Z   R   C   L   B   R
T   I   E   W   A   X   G   A   Y   I   V   R   C   U   L   I
S   N   V   R   P   E   E   Q   T   T   T   S   P   A   E   T
U   G   O   L   T   C   M   P   N   Y   R   O   L   G   S   O
J   K   C   I   I   J   A   I   E   L   D   N   A   C   S   H
F   G   H   O   S   B   Y   L   T   H   G   I   R   P   U   C
E   W   V   D   M   N   I   S   L   A   N   I   G   I   R   O
S   E   R   V   A   N   T   A   B   D   E   V   O   L   E   B
```

Answer Key: baptism, sacrament, initiation, water, candle, white garment, welcoming, original sin, community, oil, Catholic, RCIA
Isaiah: servant, justice, covenant, light
Psalm: glory, voice, bless, give
Acts: Good News, peace, Holy Spirit, upright
Luke: Messiah, John, beloved, baptize

The following activity ideas also relate to the Scripture readings. You may want to read the passage(s) indicated as part of the activity.

- Invite the young people to write a baptism prayer for children being baptized this year. Each small group could write a verse and then blend it together with what the other groups have written. Include the symbols of baptism and especially the component of being welcomed into the community. Ask a teen who knows calligraphy to write the words elegantly and ask another who is artistic to decorate the prayers with symbols of baptism. Copy them onto parchment paper and give them to the families of the children welcomed into your community by baptism. (Luke 3:15–16,21–22)

- With the New Year, invite the teens to make some resolutions about how to act more justly toward others. Ask the teens to write their resolutions in the form of a letter. Then have them address envelopes to themselves and seal the letters in the envelopes. Mail them to the young people six months later to remind them of their resolutions for justice. (Isa. 42:1–4,6–7)

- Ask the teens to answer the following question:
  ○ When I have children of my own, I would want them baptized because . . .
  (All readings)

- Invite the teens to write a letter to at least one of their godparents, asking the godparent(s) to tell them everything they can remember about the teen's baptism day. If the godparents are nearby, the teen could interview them in person. Have the teens put the letter or tape in a treasure box to share with their own children someday. (All readings)

Lent

First Sunday of Lent

Scripture Readings (24)

- ❖ Deut. 26:4–10
- ❖ Ps. 91:1–2,10–11,12–13,14–15
- ❖ Rom. 10:8–13
- ❖ Luke 4:1–13

God's Word

A major theme of the Scripture readings is "Lead us not into temptation."

The readings today ask us to examine what we believe and to avoid the temptation to stray from those beliefs.

In the first reading, Moses tells the people to celebrate their deliverance by God. This ritual of giving thanks for the harvest is a time for remembering and storytelling, and a time to celebrate, with family, God's many blessings. Moses tells the people to place a gift on the altar, the best of what they have grown in the soil of their new land. As they offer it back to God, they are to witness about how God saved them from captivity in Egypt. After bowing with respect and reverence for God, they go on to celebrate with their families.

This psalm warns us that faith does not make us immune to temptation but can help us get through tough times. Have you ever gotten yourself into trouble and not been able to find a way out? The psalmist knows that God is the way out. God is both shelter and fortress—someone to trust. We often end up in more trouble than just a stubbed toe, but just as God delivered Israel from Egypt, God is there in our personal times of distress. We are saved as individuals and as a community.

The writer of the Letter to the Romans knows that sometimes what we believe and what we say are two different things. Real Christians know God in their heart and also on their lips: they know in their heart that only God can repair the relationship between God and humans that is broken by sin, and they proclaim with their mouth how God saves them through Jesus. The second part of the reading says that although the Jews were the original inheritors of the Covenant, Jesus came to save all: "There is no difference between Jew and Greek," between rich and poor, between Americans and Russians, between black and white.

The reading from the Gospel of Luke recounts in some detail Jesus' run-in with the devil in the desert. Jesus had gone into the desert to fast and pray before beginning his public ministry in earnest. After forty days, Jesus must have been tired and hungry. Of course, the devil shows up for Jesus at the same times he shows up for us—the times when we are most vulnerable.

First, the devil tempts Jesus to turn stones into bread. Jesus knows bread is not everything, and he gives the devil a Scripture lesson. Second, the devil offers to give up his power if Jesus will worship him. The devil's next lesson from Jesus is on the Commandments—love God and God only. Finally, the devil tempts Jesus to test God's love for his Son. It is the devil who flunks this test about God's love.

Temptations are a daily fact of life. Jesus shows us how to respond to them.

Themes for Teens

The following themes from the Scriptures relate to the lives of teens:

- Leave the devil in the desert.
- Beat temptation.
- Remember and celebrate.
- The Lord gets us out of trouble.
- Believe and witness.

Lent

Our Response

Activity Leave the Devil in the Desert

This activity is keyed to the Gospel reading. It takes the simple childhood game commonly called Monkey in the Middle and turns it into an illustration of how to follow Jesus' example when we meet the devil—in the desert of our own life.

- Ask the young people to stand facing one another in a circle, which represents the Christian community. Call for a volunteer to be the first "devil" to stand in the middle of the circle. Explain that the ball used in this game represents faith, the object of the game is to pass the ball (faith) from one person to another without the devil taking it away. In other words, they are trying to "keep the faith," as the devil tries to do whatever possible to steal faith as it is tossed from person to person. If the devil temporarily steals faith away, the last person with the ball becomes the new devil for the next round of the game.

  After playing the game for a while, relate it to today's Gospel reading.
  - What can we do to avoid temptation?
  - How did Jesus show us we should treat the devil?
  - How can we ask God's help in times of temptation?

Activity Ideas The following activity ideas also relate to the Scripture readings. You may want to read the passage(s) indicated as part of the activity.

- Explain that in the first reading, the Israelites take time to remember and retell the story of their deliverance by God. In their journal, ask the teens to reflect on their own story of faith.
  - Who are some of the key characters?
  - Where are some of the key scenes?
  - How did God get you to where you are today?

  (Deut. 26:4–10)

- Sing the song "On Eagle's Wings," by Michael Joncas (*Glory and Praise* [Phoenix, AZ: North American Liturgy Resources, 1987], no. 178). Invite the teens to add hand motions to the refrain and to each verse of the song. (Ps. 91:1–2,10–11,12–13,14–15)

- Jesus fasted and prayed in the desert before beginning his public ministry. Instruct the teens to make a calendar for Lent. In each square have them write ways that they can fast, pray, or serve others while preparing for Easter. Urge them to hang their calendar up at home and to try to follow through on their Lenten intentions. (Luke 4:1–13)

- After reading the psalm, ask the young people to name some of the things and situations that get them into trouble. Lent has traditionally been a time for giving up things. Ask, Why not give up putting yourself in situations where trouble lurks? (Ps. 91:1–2,10–11,12–13,14–15)

Second Sunday of Lent

Scripture Readings (27)

- ❖ Gen. 15:5–12,17–18
- ❖ Ps. 27:1,7–8,8–9,13–14
- ❖ Phil. 3:17—4:1
- ❖ Luke 9:28–36

God's Word

A major theme of the Scripture readings is "God's promise to us."

In the first reading, we hear about Abraham, who is very old and has no land and no children. But God works wonders when things seem impossible. In a mysterious scene of sacrifice, God seals a Covenant, promising Abraham many descendants and a land to call his own. Christians see themselves as Abraham's descendants too, because Abraham is the father of faith. In this very personal encounter between God and humanity, Abraham shows a deep trust in God, a model for our own relationship with the Creator. Abraham promises to trust in God. God promises to bless and be faithful to him. Nothing we can do will make God break this promise to us, Abraham's descendants by faith.

The psalmist wants to look upon the face of God. In the light of salvation, we have nothing to fear. The psalmist, like Abraham, is called to trust in God. Even in adversity we need to stand firm in our relationship with God. We do not need to fear, for God will protect us.

In the second reading, the Philippians are told to be careful of whom they choose to imitate. The "enemies of the cross of Christ" think only of how they can rob Jesus' death of its meaning. These people try to convince Paul's congregation in Philippi of a teaching different from the one Paul gave them. Paul tells them to remember that they are destined for heaven. If they imitate Paul in good moral action and a commitment to Christ, then Christ will transform them into his glory.

Luke's Gospel reading recounts the Transfiguration of Christ. Through the appearance of Moses and Elijah, Jesus is identified as both prophet and lawgiver, but more important, as the Son of God. As Moses and Elijah talk with Jesus, they talk about his death that is about to take place in Jerusalem.

Jesus took three disciples with him when he went to pray. The disciples were so excited by what they saw that they wanted the moment to last forever. They were ready to pitch tents for a camp. Moses and Elijah point to the "exodus" of Jesus, but the disciples didn't know that this journey was still to come. The message from God rings loud and clear for us, as it did for the disciples that day: "'This is my Son, my Chosen One: Listen to him.'"

Themes for Teens

The following themes from the Scriptures relate to the lives of teens:
- God keeps promises.
- God is our light.
- Look toward heaven.
- We are transformed with Jesus.
- Listen to Jesus.

Our Response

Activity

The Light of Our Salvation

This craft project invites the young people to share the light of God's salvation as celebrated in Psalm 27 by making a candle as a gift for a loved one.

You will need paraffin wax, old crayons, empty coffee cans, small milk cartons, crushed ice, and heavy string for this project.

Melt the paraffin wax in a coffee can over very low heat. Stir in old crayons to color the wax. Cut string for wicks at least three inches longer than the candle. Soak the string in melted paraffin until it hardens straight.

Cut the top off of the milk carton and poke a hole in the bottom of it to pull the waxed string through. Tie the other end to a pencil to hold it in the center.

Fill the carton with crushed ice. Quickly fill the rest of the carton with the melted wax. Allow it to harden at least overnight. Drain the water from the carton and then remove the carton carefully.

Invite the teens to give the candle to someone as a gift, along with a copy of today's psalm.

Activity Ideas

The following activity ideas also relate to the Scripture readings. You may want to read the passage(s) indicated as part of the activity.

- In the first reading, Abraham trusts God to fulfill a promise made to him and his descendants. Pair off the teens and ask them to do a trust fall. One teen stands behind the other. The one standing in front is to fall backward and trust that the one behind will catch her or him. Switch places and repeat. Make sure you have spotters so that no one gets hurt. Discuss: Why is it hard to trust that the other person will catch you? Why is it even tougher sometimes to trust that God will catch us when we fall? (Gen. 15:5–12,17–18)

- In the second reading, we are told to imitate Christ. Ask the young people to list some of the things Jesus did—heal the sick, forgive sinners, preach the Good News, still the wind and waves, gather little children, and so on. Divide the teens into groups of four. Ask each group to choose one of the examples of Jesus' actions and prepare a mime presentation of it. When they are ready, ask one group at a time to present its "Jesus action" without a word or sound. Invite the other teens to identify from each presentation the way we can imitate Christ. (Phil. 3:17—4:1)

- In the Gospel passage, the voice of God tells us to listen to Jesus. How well does your group listen? At the time when your meeting should start, proclaim the Gospel, but without asking everyone to be quiet. After you are done, give each of the teens a pencil and a piece of paper and ask them to write down everything they heard. Some may have little or nothing on their paper. Talk about the many distractions in our lives—from other people and from our own thoughts—that sometimes make it too noisy for us to listen to and understand the Scripture readings during Mass. Ask: What can we do to try to tune out distractions and tune in the Good News? (Luke 9:28–36)

- In their journal, ask the teens to describe, through the eyes of one of the disciples who went with Jesus up the mountain, what happened during the Transfiguration in today's Gospel passage. It could begin with: "You'll never believe what I saw . . ." (Luke 9:28–36)

Third Sunday of Lent

Scripture Readings
(30)

❖ Exod. 3:1–8,13–15
❖ Ps. 103:1–2,3–4,6–7,8,11
❖ 1 Cor. 10:1–6,10–12
❖ Luke 13:1–9

God's Word

A major theme of the Scripture readings is "Reform your ways."

In the first reading, Moses is out watching his father-in-law's flock when God decides to get his attention. God sets a bush on fire, and it keeps burning and burning, even after all the branches should have been ashes. God calls Moses by name and tells him to take off his shoes because he is standing on holy ground. God tells Moses that the Israelites have suffered enough in captivity, and that Moses is to be God's messenger and lead the people to freedom. Moses wants to know who is sending him on this great quest. God says, "'I am who am.'"

This psalm is reassuring during the season of the year when we are mindful of our sins and seek forgiveness from God. We see not a judge or a prison warden but a God who is slow to anger, kind, and merciful. The psalmist praises God's name, for our sins and the sins of the community will be forgiven. God's ability to forgive and keep forgiving is beyond all human understanding.

In this letter Paul teaches a history lesson to the Corinthians. Even after God delivers the Israelites from Egypt, they still betray God by worshiping idols. They become lazy and complacent and forget all that God has done for them. We are told to learn from their example, because all our actions have consequences. The last line of this reading reminds us not to become lazy or overconfident, because that's exactly when we will fall.

In the reading from Luke, some people come to ask Jesus about a tragedy that has happened to some Galileans who have been killed and their blood sacrificed to the Roman gods. Jesus tries to correct their mistaken idea that people who experience such disasters and accidents are sinners. At the same time, Jesus warns them to take a close look at their lives and to reform their ways because sin will be punished.

Jesus then tells the parable of the fig tree, combining a call to reform with a message of hope. Would you keep a fruit tree in your yard if it never gave you any fruit? The vinedresser in the parable continues to care for the fig tree just as God continues to care for us when we sin. Lent is a good time to examine the fruit of our life and to ask God's help to prune away the dead branches so that we can bear fruit again.

Themes for Teens

The following themes from the Scriptures relate to the lives of teens:
• Reform your ways.
• Stand on holy ground.
• Bear some fruit.
• Is your life fruitless?
• Don't fall for judging others.

Lent

Our Response

Activity

The Lord Is Kind and Merciful

This prayer intersperses today's psalm response with stories of forgiveness found in the Scriptures.

- *Call to prayer.* "Then Peter came and said to [Jesus], 'Lord, if [my brother] sins against me, how often should I forgive? As many as seven times?' Jesus said to him, 'Not seven times, but, I tell you, seventy [times] seven'" (Matt. 18:21–22, NRSV).
- *Sung response.* The Lord is kind and merciful, the Lord is kind and merciful.
- *Left side.* "'Which is easier, to say to the paralytic, "Your sins are forgiven," or to say, "Stand up and take your mat and walk"? But so that you may know that the Son of Man has authority on earth to forgive sins'"—[Jesus] said to the paralytic—"'I say to you, stand up, take your mat and go to your home'" (Mark 2:9–11).
- *Sung response.* The Lord is kind and merciful, the Lord is kind and merciful.
- *Right side.* "'When [the shepherd] has found [his lost sheep], he lays it on his shoulders and rejoices. And when he comes home, he calls together his friends and neighbors, saying to them, "Rejoice with me, for I have found my sheep that was lost." Just so, I tell you, there will be more joy in heaven over one sinner who repents than over ninety-nine righteous persons who need no repentance'" (Luke 15:5–7).
- *Sung response.* The Lord is kind and merciful, the Lord is kind and merciful.
- *Left side.* "'So he set off and went to his father. But while he was still far off, his father saw him and was filled with compassion; he ran and put his arms around him and kissed him. Then the son said to him, "Father, I have sinned against heaven and before you; I am no longer worthy to be called your son." But the father said to his slaves, "Quickly, bring out a robe—the best one—and put it on him; put a ring on his finger and sandals on his feet. And get the fatted calf and kill it, and let us eat and celebrate; for this son of mine was dead and is alive again; he was lost and is found!" And they began to celebrate'" (Luke 15:20–24).
- *Sung response.* The Lord is kind and merciful, the Lord is kind and merciful.
- *Right side.* "'"Let anyone among you who is without sin be the first to throw a stone at her." And once again he bent down and wrote on the ground. When they heard it, they went away, one by one, beginning with the elders; and Jesus was left alone with the woman standing before him. Jesus straightened up and said to her, "Woman, where are they? Has no one condemned you?" She said, "No one, sir." And Jesus said, "Neither do I condemn you. Go your way, and from now on do not sin again"'" (John 8:7–11).
- *Sung response.* The Lord is kind and merciful, the Lord is kind and merciful.
- *Left side.* "Jesus said, 'Father, forgive them; for they do not know what they are doing'" (Luke 23:34).
- *Sung response.* The Lord is kind and merciful, the Lord is kind and merciful.
- *Right side.* "Jesus said to them again, 'Peace be with you. As the Father has sent me, so I send you.' . . . 'If you forgive the sins of any, they are forgiven them; if you retain the sins of any, they are retained'" (John 20:21,23).
- *Sung response.* The Lord is kind and merciful, the Lord is kind and merciful.
- *Closing prayer.* "Then Peter came and said to [Jesus], 'Lord, if [my brother] sins against me, how often should I forgive? As many as seven times?' Jesus said to him, 'Not seven times, but, I tell you, seventy [times] seven'" (Matt. 18:21–22).

<table>
<tr><td align="right">Activity Ideas</td><td>The following activity ideas also relate to the Scripture readings. You may want to read the passage(s) indicated as part of the activity.</td></tr>
</table>

- Invite a master gardener to give the teens a brief lesson on how to prune trees and why they must be pruned to grow better. If possible, allow the teens to help prune some trees that can be pruned at this time of the year in your part of the country. You may even want to visit a gardening center for your lesson and later bring a fruit tree home to plant on your parish or school property. The teens can take care of it until the tree bears fruit. Later, invite the teens to reflect on the following: What branches do you need to prune from your tree? How can you bear fruit for God and others? (Luke 13:1–9)

- At the start of your meeting, get the attention of the teens by doing something unusual, such as popping a balloon, wearing a funny mask, or having some pop-up trick snakes jump out of a can. In the first reading, God sets a bush on fire to get Moses' attention. Ask the teens what God does in their life to try to get their attention. Contrast the burning bush in the first reading to the dying fig tree in the Gospel reading. Ask: "Are you more like a burning bush or a dying fig tree?" (Exod. 3:1–8,13–15; Luke 13:1–9)

- Divide the young people into groups of eight. Pass an orange around the circle. As each teen pulls a small part of the peel away, and before passing the orange to the next person, ask her or him to complete the following sentence: "I can bear fruit by . . ."

  By the end of the discussion, all the orange peel should be peeled away, and the teens can enjoy eating a fruit of God's creation for a snack. (Luke 13:1–9)

- Moses asked for a name to describe God. Challenge the teens to design a business card for God. Make sure the card includes name, title, and company logo. (Exod. 3:1–8,13–15)

- Urge the teens to find a comfortable spot in their house, put on some soothing music, take off their shoes, sit on the floor, and relax. Then have them ask themselves, "What am I going to do with my 'holy ground'?" (Exod. 3:1–8,13–15)

Fourth Sunday of Lent

<table>
<tr><td align="right">Scripture Readings
(33)</td><td>❖ Jos. 5:9,10–12
❖ Ps. 34:2–3,4–5,6–7
❖ 2 Cor. 5:17–21
❖ Luke 15:1–3,11–32</td></tr>
</table>

<table>
<tr><td align="right">God's Word</td><td>A major theme of the Scripture readings is "Coming home."

    This reading from Joshua is about the first celebration of the Passover feast, in which the Jews mark their deliverance by God from bondage to freedom. While the people are on their journey, God provides manna from heaven for them to eat. When they arrive in their new land, God continues to provide for them, giving them fertile land so that they can grow their own</td></tr>
</table>

food to eat. Coming home to their new land is a sign of reconciliation between the people and their God. Their celebration of deliverance is still celebrated as Passover by most Jews today.

The psalmist appeals to our senses to encourage us to praise our God. We need to pray from our experiences. We are not only to praise God for what we see, but also to taste and touch and hear God's goodness. We grow in our relationship with God through the wonder of our everyday encounters with God's creation.

In the Second Letter to the Corinthians, Paul explains that Jesus is the new Passover. The forgiveness of God gives each of us a new lease on life—a chance to start over again, to become a new creation. Christ brings the message of reconciliation to the world and restores our relationship with God and with the community. Just as the Israelites in the first reading were freed from captivity, Jesus delivers us from the bondage of sin to the freedom of forgiveness. We are called to extend this gift of reconciliation to others.

In the Gospel of Luke, we learn that the Pharisees and scribes are not happy with Jesus because he was hanging out with sinners. Their grumbling prompts Jesus to tell one of the most beloved stories of forgiveness in the Scriptures:

> A man had two sons. The younger one got impatient, wanted his cut of the inheritance even while his father was still alive. After getting the money, he took off and squandered everything, living the high life. The older son stayed home by the father's side. Left to tend pigs and even eat with them, the younger son saw the error of his ways. He headed home to apologize and hoped his dad would hire him as an extra servant. Not only did his dad forgive him, but the son got a hero's welcome, the best clothes, and a grand feast. This did not go over too well with the other brother. He got angry and stomped off. But his dad went to him and let him know that he, too, was loved. The father coaxed him into joining the celebration for his brother who was dead and has come back to life, who was lost and is found. (Adapted from Luke 15:11–24)

God shows deep and constant love for us no matter what we do. God is the loving, compassionate father who reaches out to both the loyal son and the lost son.

Themes for Teens The following themes from the Scriptures relate to the lives of teens:
- God sets his people free.
- Experience God's goodness.
- God lets us start over.
- Forgive as God forgives.
- We can always come home.

Our Response

Activity ### Walk with the Prodigal

This activity is keyed to the Gospel reading. Show "The Prodigal Son," from *God's Trombones: A Trilogy of African-American Poems,* written by James Weldon Johnson. The video is available from Billy Budd Films. See page 144 for their address and phone number.

After watching the video, allow 5 minutes for the teens to reflect on it. After the quiet time, ask the teens to pair up and discuss the following:
- Imagine that you are the son walking back home. What is going through your head? How do you feel?
- Later, in the midst of your welcome-home party, what is going through your head? How do you feel?

Activity Ideas

The following activity ideas also relate to the Scripture readings. You may want to read the passage(s) indicated as part of the activity.

- Have the young people form several small groups. Divide today's Gospel parable into sections and give one section to each small group. Ask the groups to write three questions for an examination of conscience to match their part of the story. For example, after reading of the younger son's demands, questions could include:
  - Do I make too many demands of my parents?
  - Do I ask for things I don't really need?
  - Do I waste some of the gifts that God has given to me?

  Gather the groups together for a prayerful reading of the Gospel, interspersed with an examination of conscience. If possible, give the teens an opportunity to individually receive the sacrament of reconciliation. (Luke 15:1–3,11–32)

- Prepare the traditional Seder plate for Passover, and share the meaning with your group of teens.
  - *Karpas,* a mild vegetable such as parsley or celery, is dipped into salt water or vinegar. The parsley symbolizes spring. The salt water symbolizes the tears of the Israelites in captivity.
  - *Maror,* a bitter herb—usually horseradish—symbolizes the bitterness of slavery for the Jews.
  - *Hazeret,* another bitter herb—sometimes watercress or romaine lettuce—is another reminder of slavery.
  - *Haroset,* a sweet spread of fruit, nuts, and wine, symbolizes the mortar and mud bricks that the slaves used to build Pharaoh's cities.
  - *Zeroah,* a roasted shank bone, symbolizes the paschal lamb. On the eve of the Exodus, the blood of the lamb was used to mark the doorposts of the Israelites.
  - *Baytzah,* a roasted egg, is a symbol of mourning for the loss of the Holy Temple.

  (Adapted from Greene, *The Jewish Holiday Cookbook,* pp. 238–239)
  (Jos. 5:9,10–12)

- After reflecting on the first reading, ask the young people to journal on the following topic: "How does God feed you physically? How does God feed you spiritually?" (Jos. 5:9,10–12)

- Invite the teens to explore some of the feelings associated with sin and forgiveness.
  - How do you feel when you sin?
  - How do you feel when you are forgiven?
  - How do you feel like a new creation after receiving the sacrament of reconciliation?

  (All readings)

Lent

Fifth Sunday of Lent

Scripture Readings (36)

- ❖ Isa. 43:16–21
- ❖ Ps. 126:1–2,2–3,4–5,6
- ❖ Phil. 3:8–14
- ❖ John 8:1–11

God's Word

A major theme of the Scripture readings is "God is always with us."

Water plays an important role in the first reading today. The first part of the reading recounts God parting the Red Sea so that the Israelites could pass safely through the water during their flight from captivity in Egypt. Later, the water swallows up their Egyptian pursuers. God triumphs over the sea and the Egyptians. They are no match for God. God is also described as life-giving water in the dryness of the desert. We need water to survive. We need God to survive.

When the Israelites taste freedom at last, it seems too good to be true. They are sure that they're dreaming. Tears dissolve into rejoicing. Seeds grow quickly and produce sheaves full of grain. This celebration psalm calls everyone to rejoice in God's many blessings.

In his Letter to the Philippians, Paul writes that he has discovered what is most important—making Christ the center of his life. Paul is excited about the impact of Christ on his life. Yet, to know Christ closely, we must set aside all the clutter of unimportant things that get in the way. Former accomplishments seem insignificant. Former wealth is called "rubbish." Nothing else matters much once we find Jesus. In the second part of the reading, Paul describes himself running toward the finish line. Like a runner in training for the Olympics, concentration and determination keep us on the path to life in Jesus.

In today's Gospel reading, the Pharisees bring to Jesus a woman accused of adultery. They remind Jesus that Moses' punishment for such a crime was stoning, a death penalty. Jesus does not give them an answer right away but begins tracing with his finger in the dirt. No one is sure what Jesus was writing. Some believe he was writing a list of sins of the woman's accusers. Then Jesus looks up and says, "'Let the man among you who has no sin be the first to cast a stone.'" One by one, the startled challengers drop their rocks and go away. When all are gone, Jesus forgives the woman and tells her to sin no more.

Themes for Teens

The following themes from the Scriptures relate to the lives of teens:
- Do not judge others.
- Jesus is our finish line.
- Run the race with Jesus.
- Celebrate God's gifts.
- Even the sea obeys God.

Our Response

Activity   Drawing in the Sand

This activity is keyed to the Gospel reading. It invites the young people to explore the richness of the symbols of rocks and sandy dirt found in today's reading. It helps them to better understand how it feels to be forgiven by Jesus and how we need to let go of some of our sinful ways as we journey closer to Easter.

Ask the teens to read today's Gospel passage in small groups.

Give each group a one-minute egg timer filled with sand. Only the person holding the timer may speak. As sand flows though the timer, each young person has 1 minute to share what he or she thinks Jesus was writing in the sand in today's Gospel reading.

Create a makeshift sandbox by filling a small plastic swimming pool with at least three inches of sand. Ask the young people to think of one word to describe how they feel after seeing Jesus' forgiveness in action in this Gospel passage. Tell them to quietly write that feeling word in the sand with their finger.

Give each teen a medium-size rock. Try to find rocks that have at least one smooth surface. Using markers, ask the teens to write on a rock one thing they need to leave behind before they can embrace Easter as it nears.

At the end of the meeting, ask the teens to leave the rocks behind at the foot of the cross—either one already present in your worship space for the season of Lent, or one you have set up in your prayer space specifically for this meeting.

Activity Ideas

The following activity ideas also relate to the Scripture readings. You may want to read the passage(s) indicated as part of the activity.

- After reading today's Gospel, give each teen a small stone. Ask the teens to put it in their locker at school, put it on their dresser at home, or carry it in their pocket as a reminder when they feel like throwing stones (or cruel words or fists) at someone. (John 8:1–11)

- Read today's first reading together. Rent the video *The Ten Commandments,* starring Charlton Heston. Show the scene where God parts the Red Sea so that the Israelites can pass through it. Make sure you include the fate of the Egyptians who try to follow after them. Talk about how the Israelites must have felt after this great miracle. Close by praying today's psalm together. (Isa. 43:16–21; Ps. 126:1–2,2–3,4–5,6)

- Divide the teens into teams to compete in a series of races or relay games. At the end, award each team a small trophy inscribed with the words "Life in Jesus." Ask the teens what they have learned about today's second reading from this activity. (Phil. 3:8–14)

- In the second reading, Paul describes how Jesus has become the center of his life. Invite the teens to sing "Center of My Life," by Paul Inwood (*Gather* [Chicago: GIA Publications, 1988], no. 251). After the first verse, pause for the teens to offer ways that God is their refuge. After the second verse, invite them to share ways that God gives advice or direction. After the third, have them offer reasons to rejoice in God. After verse four, tell them to ask God for help to follow Jesus' path of life. (Phil. 3:8–14)

- In teams, ask the teens to make a list of top prizes and awards, for example, the Nobel Peace Prize, an academy award, a Pulitzer Prize, a Super Bowl ring, an Olympic gold medal, and so on. See which group has the longest list after 10 minutes. Discuss how these awards pale in comparison to Jesus, the prize at the finish line. (Phil. 3:8–14)

Palm Sunday

Scripture Readings (38)

- ❖ Isa. 50:4–7
- ❖ Ps. 22:8–9,17–18,19–20,23–24
- ❖ Phil. 2:6–11
- ❖ Luke 22:14—23:56

God's Word

A major theme of the Scripture readings is "The suffering of God's servants."

In the Book of Isaiah, we find a person who has been faithful and trusting toward God despite people who beat him and make fun of him. Like all prophets, this one suffers abuse in the name of God. He perseveres because he knows it is not a disgrace to serve God. This image of a suffering servant is later applied to Jesus Christ, who fulfills the role of Suffering Servant of God.

The psalm continues the theme of hope despite persecution. The writer cries out, wondering why he is left alone to suffer. Here, too, the verses sound much like the suffering that Jesus endured on the cross, as recorded in the Gospel reading of the Passion. We read of pierced hands and of casting lots for garments. The verses present a sharp contrast between honor and humiliation—a lot like this Sunday's liturgy, with Jesus' triumphant procession of palms being followed by his death on the cross. Yet the psalmist continues to praise and give glory to God. Even in the depths of despair, we can trust in God.

In Philippians, we learn that Jesus did not hold on to his position as God. Instead, he humbled himself to be one of us and to die like one of us. But in accepting the humiliation of the cross, God exalted him and made him Lord of all.

In the reading of the Passion, we walk with Jesus through his suffering and death. It is draining, not so much because it is long, but more so because of the strong feelings it stirs within us.

Here is a brief outline of the chain of events: Jesus breaks the bread of his body and shares the wine of his blood at his last Passover meal with his friends. He struggles with his fate as he prays in the garden and then is abandoned by the disciples closest to him. One of them betrays Jesus to the authorities. Another one of his closest friends, Peter, saves himself by denying Jesus not once, but three times. Although earlier a crowd had followed Jesus through the streets with palms, singing his praises, now another crowd rejects him in favor of a criminal. When charged with being the King of the Jews, Jesus gives no defense and is sentenced to death. After Jesus has suffered terrible beatings, Simon of Cyrene carries Jesus' cross to the place of death. Jesus is nailed to the cross like a common criminal. After the agony of his death, he is buried in someone else's tomb.

Themes for Teens

The following themes from the Scriptures relate to the lives of teens:
- The Lord is my help.
- God will not abandon us.
- Jesus Christ is Lord.
- Jesus sacrificed himself for us.
- We stand by the cross.

Our Response

Activity   You Are Invited

This activity is keyed to the readings as a whole. Most youth groups and classes do not meet during Holy Week. This activity is a way to encourage the young people to participate fully in the Holy Week services in their parish communities.

Send each teen in your youth group or class the following handwritten, personalized invitation:

> [Name of teen],
> Jesus of Nazareth
> requests the honor of your presence
> at a dinner to be held
> in his honor.

Include in each invitation a copy of the Holy Week schedule at each teen's parish. If you are all from the same parish, you may want to invite the teens and their families to sit together at some of the liturgies.

Activity Ideas

The following activity ideas also relate to the Scripture readings. You may want to read the passage(s) indicated as part of the activity.

- Gather the young people together to pray the stations of the cross as a community. You may want to use the booklet "The Way of the Cross for Young Christians," by Rev. William J. McLoughlin, available from Barton-Cotton, 1405 Parker Road, Baltimore, MD 21227, 301-247-4800. Ask a different teen to lead the prayer at each station. You may want to check with area retreat centers to see if anyone has outdoor stations and arrange a field trip. (All readings)

- Invite the teens to help with the Palm Sunday and Holy Week liturgies. On Palm Sunday they could give out palms to parishioners or lead children in the procession at the beginning of the liturgy. On Holy Thursday they could help wash feet or provide the water or towels for each station. On Good Friday they could carry a large cross into the worship space and hold it during the veneration of the cross. And on Holy Saturday they could bring baskets of food to be blessed before giving them to needy families. (All readings)

- Find someone in your parish who knows the tradition of weaving palms into crosses. Ask this person to show the teens how to weave a cross and to explain why he or she continues this tradition. Urge the teens to hang their cross in their room until the next Ash Wednesday, when the palm will be burned. (Luke 22:14—23:56)

- One of the things that distinguishes Luke's account of the Passion from those of the other Gospel writers is his attention to the women mourners. Ask the teens to read through the Passion to find the women mentioned in the reading. What were they doing? How did they participate in the events unfolding? How do you think they felt about what was happening? (Luke 22:14—23:56)

Lent

Easter

Easter Sunday

Scripture Readings (43)

- ❖ Acts 10:34,37–43
- ❖ Ps. 118:1–2,16–17,22–23
- ❖ Col. 3:1–4
- ❖ John 20:1–9

God's Word

A major theme of the Scripture readings is "The tomb is empty."

Peter's speech from the Acts of the Apostles provides a short overview of Jesus' life, mission, and death. It reads like a news report of Jesus' life, from his roots in Nazareth to his Resurrection. The cross becomes a symbol of victory rather than a symbol of death. The people are called to be witnesses to this great legacy.

The psalm allows us to put away the melancholy of Lent and sing the alleluias of Easter. This is a great day, a day made by the Lord. A stone, once rejected by the builders, has become the stone the entire building rests on. Jesus, rejected by the leaders of Israel, is now risen and becomes the center of a whole new faith. Rejoice and be glad. We are saved by God and live triumphant over death.

In Colossians we are told that we, too, have been raised up with Christ. However, new life requires a new way of living. We are to set aside things of this earth and look to the things of heaven. We are to leave behind the old ways of death and participate in the new life of Easter.

The Gospel reading takes us right to the tomb on the first Easter morning. Day has hardly broken. Mary Magdalene goes to the tomb to find it empty. She runs to get the others. All they find are burial wrappings—no Jesus.

No one expects the Resurrection, despite all Jesus had foretold about it. They expect Jesus to still be lying in the tomb. Even when they have seen the empty tomb, their first thought is that someone has stolen his body.

To celebrate Easter is to remember that Jesus still lives and walks among us. The tomb is empty; Jesus is alive!

Themes for Teens

The following themes from the Scriptures relate to the lives of teens:
- If we believe, our sins are forgiven.
- Celebrate! Jesus lives!
- Alleluia!
- We rise again with Christ.
- The tomb is empty.

Our Response

Activity

Easter Eggs for Jesus

This family activity is keyed to all the readings. It combines the secular tradition of coloring eggs at Easter time with a powerful poem celebrating Jesus' life, death, and Resurrection.

Give each family an inexpensive egg-coloring kit and ask them to share the following poem as they color eggs this year, pausing during the reading after stanzas 3 to 13 and stanza 15 to color the egg that goes with each stanza.

Easter Eggs for Jesus

Here's a dozen eggs for Easter,
fresh, large, and Grade A too;
to tell the glorious story
in all the rainbow hues.

Let's color eggs for Jesus, then
violet, orange, and red.
And celebrate God's Easter when
Jesus rose from the dead.

Let's dye the first egg stubborn gray,
for the shaggy donkey on its way.
Until Jesus lay upon the hay,
the world was wrapped in gloomy gray.

Let's brush the second egg soft blush pink,
pink as a baby's tender flesh;
for when Jesus was born of a virgin girl
the sad gray world was blessed.

Let's splash the third egg in cool, wet blue
like the river, lake, and sea;
for Jesus, baptized in the Jordan,
taught God's law on Lake Galilee.

Let's wash the fourth egg lily white,
clean as bath soap and ivory like a dove;
for Jesus, the gentle Lamb of God,
without blemish, was God's Beloved.

Let's brush the fifth egg vibrant green,
gorgeous as the grass color;
where Jesus fed five thousand folks,
and led them to lush pasture.

Let's dip the sixth egg in bright yellow,
for the cheerful flower there;
that neither toiled or spun all day,
but blossomed in praise and prayer.

Let's dye the seventh egg deep purple,
like the crushed grapes from the vine,
for Jesus forgave our painful sins
with the sweetness of new wine.

Let's coat the eighth egg in a golden hue,
like the wheat and the grain it yields;
for Jesus is the truest Bread of Life,
and the best treasure in the field.

Let's paint the ninth egg solid brown,
as brown as the crude cut tree,
which Jesus hung and died upon;
the cross, for you and me.

Let's soak the tenth egg in rich thick red,
as red as his precious blood,
that poured from his holy hands and side,
and stained the rugged wood.

Let's polish the eleventh egg shiny crow black,
as black as a coal mine shaft;
for when Jesus was buried in the earth
everything was dark as that.

The universe was devoid of joy,
and the world was spelled with doom,
for all colors emptied into night,
when the good Lord was entombed.

Let's glaze the twelfth egg brilliant orange,
like a thousand suns ablaze,
which torched the darkness on Easter morn
when Christ the Lord was raised.

The Light of Life streamed from the grave
as paint poured over creation;
so the Earth was one huge Easter egg,
God colored with salvation.

Here's a dozen eggs for Easter, friends
all colored to God's glory;
like the twelve disciples Jesus sent
to tell the Gospel story.

Let's give great praise to Jesus, then,
in aqua, fuchsia, gold;
And our lives to serve and honor him,
beautiful, and bold.

(Martinson, *Parish Teacher,* p. 14)

Activity Ideas

The following activity ideas also relate to the Scripture readings. You may want to read the passage(s) indicated as part of the activity.

- Invite the young people to go along with eucharistic ministers who take the Eucharist to those who cannot attend Mass on Easter morning. Ask the teens to join in prayer with the shut-in. Perhaps each teen can bring some Easter flowers to cheer the person as well. (All readings)

- Before Easter, ask the teens to fill plastic Easter eggs with the message "Jesus lives, Alleluia." After the Mass they attend with their family on Easter Sunday, station the young people at each door after Mass to hand out eggs to the children as a reminder that Easter is much more than eating chocolate bunnies. (All readings)

- In their journal, ask the teens to walk in the shoes of Mary Magdalene on that first Easter and write what she must have been thinking and feeling as she found the tomb empty that morning. (John 20:1–9)

- The psalm rejoices, "This is the day the Lord has made; let us rejoice and be glad." At Easter dinner with their family, encourage the teens to lead this psalm as the prayer before the meal, asking family members to each share one blessing they rejoice in this Easter Sunday. (Ps. 118:1–2,16–17,22–23)

Second Sunday of Easter

**Scripture Readings
(46)**

❖ Acts 5:12–16
❖ Ps. 118:2–4,13–15,22–24
❖ Rev. 1:9–11,12–13,17–19
❖ John 20:19–31

God's Word

A major theme of the Scripture readings is "Jesus in the flesh."

In Acts of the Apostles we see how the Holy Spirit continues the work of Jesus through the Apostles. The Apostles share their faith, gather the community together, and heal the sick. More and more people come to know Jesus and become Christians. People bring the sick to wherever the Apostles meet. Even people from outside Jerusalem come—and all are healed. Through the Spirit, the church grows in faith.

The psalm is a prayer of thanksgiving for God's mercy. The first verse emphasizes again and again that God's mercy endures forever. The psalmist finds courage in the Lord even when the psalmist feels he is falling. Again we hear, like last week, that the cornerstone that was once rejected is now the most essential of all.

In the second reading, the author of the Book of Revelation has the first of several visions revealing the glory of God. In the vision, he sees Jesus in post-Easter glory. Jesus is the fulfillment of the prophets. The seven lamps hark back to the words of Zechariah, and the restored remnant to the Book of Daniel. Jesus is called the first and the last and the one with authority over all creation. As the vision continues, this Christian named John is told to share the Good News with seven churches. He receives his mission to put the Good News into writing.

In last Sunday's Gospel reading, Jesus' followers found an empty tomb, with no sign of Jesus. In this Sunday's reading, Jesus comes to his followers later that night and stands before them, even though the doors are locked. The first words Jesus says are, "'Peace be with you.'" As additional evidence that it is really he who suffered and died, he shows them the wounds in his hands and side. Then Jesus sends them forth to forgive the sins of others. He promises them the gift of the Holy Spirit so that they will be the "flesh" of Jesus to carry on his mission.

Thomas isn't there the first time Jesus appears, and he has trouble believing what he is told. A week later Jesus appears again with the same greeting, "'Peace be with you.'" Jesus shows Thomas his wounds. At once, Thomas confesses his faith. Jesus blesses those who believe without seeing—Christians such as ourselves.

Themes for Teens

The following themes from the Scriptures relate to the lives of teens:
- The Spirit builds the church.
- God will love us forever.
- Make Jesus your vision.
- Peace be with you.
- Do not doubt. See and believe.

Our Response

Behind Closed Doors

This activity is keyed to the Gospel reading. It invites the young people to place themselves in the locked upper room with the disciples. It asks them to think of ways we can give one another courage to open the door and share the Good News.

Cover completely with newsprint the inside of the doors to your gathering space. After all the teens have arrived, lock the doors. Assign each group a door. If your meeting space has only one door, attach the newsprint to the wall. Ask the teens in each group to write on the door poster with markers their answers to this question: How do doubts like Thomas's prevent us from really living as Christians? When finished, ask the teens to share their answers in large groups.

Next, ask the young people for examples of ways they can give one another courage to share the Good News of Jesus' Resurrection. As each teen offers an answer, give him or her a colorful metal key attached to some yarn. Invite the teens to take the key pendants home as a reminder that Jesus holds the key to their heart, and that through his Resurrection he has given us the keys to the Kingdom of God.

Activity Ideas

The following activity ideas also relate to the Scripture readings. You may want to read the passage(s) indicated as part of the activity.

- When Thomas was convinced Jesus stood before him in the flesh, he professed, "My Lord and my God!" Ask the teens to tape this "mirror mantra" to the mirror in their bedroom or bathroom at home. Ask them to pray this mantra every time they see it on the mirror for the next week. (John 20:19–31)

- As the teens come into your meeting place, greet each one with comments such as these: "Something is different." "Did you get a haircut?" "Did you get new glasses?" Today's readings show the strong effect of Jesus' life on individuals, such as John and Thomas, and on the Christian community, the Apostles and the early church. Ask individual teens to reflect quietly on the question, "How has the Resurrection of Jesus changed you?" Pose this question to the group: "How has the Resurrection of Jesus changed us as a group?" (All readings)

- The Apostles were frightened and hid behind locked doors before the resurrected Jesus appeared among them with his blessing of peace. Pray together this beautiful prayer we share every time we celebrate the Eucharist: "Keep us from fear, undo worry and anxiety as we wait in joyful hope for the coming of our Savior, Jesus Christ." (John 20:19–31)

- In the first reading, one of the ways the Apostles continue the ministry of Jesus is to heal the sick. Because anointing of the sick is often one of the most unfamiliar sacraments to teens, explain the basics of the rite: prayer, rite of forgiveness, Scripture reading, laying on of hands, anointing with oil on forehead and hands, and receiving the Eucharist. Ask if any teen has received the sacrament or has been present as another was anointed. If so, ask how she or he felt about the experience. (Acts 5:12–16)

Easter

Third Sunday of Easter

**Scripture Readings
(49)**

- ❖ Acts 5:27–32,40–41
- ❖ Ps. 30:2,4,5–6,11–12,13
- ❖ Rev. 5:11–14
- ❖ John 21:1–19

God's Word

A major theme of the Scripture readings is "A forgiving love."

In this reading from Acts, we see the Apostles living out the mission given to them by Jesus, despite growing hostility from the authorities. The Apostles have been preaching the Good News of Jesus throughout all of Jerusalem. The high priest has already told them once to stop talking about Jesus. The popularity of the Apostles' teaching about Jesus certainly makes the high priest and those with him uncomfortable because they are to blame for Jesus' death. When the high priest confronts the Apostles with their acts of defiant evangelization, they say, "Better for us to obey God than men!" The Apostles are ordered again not to talk about Jesus and are released. Rather than be afraid, they react with joy, for they are doing the work of Jesus.

Today's psalm praises God, our rescuer and lifeguard. The writer has been through rough times, perhaps imprisoned by enemies. The experience is so frightening as to be compared to a visit to the netherworld. But God—here addressed as helper—turns mourning into dancing. The psalmist promises not to forget what God has done and to praise God forever.

This week's vision from the Book of Revelation portrays Jesus as the Lamb of God who seems to have been slain. The imagery of the lamb may come from the Passover lamb. The Lamb only *seems* to have been slain, because it has triumphed over death. Believers, too, can pass over adversity with Jesus and reach eternal life. This vision sees a new heaven and a new earth and a glorious future for those who struggle in the here and now. All creation—on heaven, on earth, and in the sea—praises God.

In the Gospel reading, the disciples are fishing when Jesus appears for the third time, although they do not recognize him at first. They had fished all night, but did not have any luck catching fish. Jesus calls from the shore and tells them where to cast their nets. When the disciples pull the nets in, they are filled nearly to breaking with fish. When the disciples recognize Jesus, Peter is so excited that he jumps into the water to reach Jesus before the others bring the boat into shore.

After Jesus cooks breakfast for them, Peter has a chance to redeem himself. Peter had denied Jesus three times. Jesus asks Peter three times, "'Do you love me?'" Each time, Peter says, "'Yes, Lord, you know that I love you.'" Jesus tells Peter to tend his lambs and feed his sheep.

Jesus ends by warning all of the death they will suffer for his sake and then renews the invitation, "'Follow me.'"

We, too, share in the mission Jesus gave Peter and the disciples—the mission to be fishers of the faithful and to tend to the other sheep in the flock. We, too, often fail to recognize Jesus at first, but we can always find him by sharing bread in the Eucharist. Like Peter, we often deny Jesus—though not always in such a dramatic way—and are in need of forgiveness. We accept Jesus' forgiveness and begin to lead a forgiving life in our relationships with others.

Themes for Teens   The following themes from the Scriptures relate to the lives of teens:
- Obey God first.
- God is our lifeguard.
- Jesus is the Lamb of God.
- Get out of the boat; come to the shore.
- Catch my fish; feed my lambs.

Our Response

Activity

Gospel Journal Writing

These journal-writing questions invite the young people to reflect more closely on several themes found in today's Gospel reading, including evangelization, forgiveness, outreach, discipleship, and Jesus' presence.

Ask the young people to read today's Gospel again when they get home and to spend some time reflecting on the following questions in their journal:

- *Cast your net.* Do you know any teens who are not part of the regular crowd, who do not come to youth group? Write some of their names in your journal. How can you cast the net of friendship wider to include them and make them feel welcome at youth group?
- *Come and eat.* Like the Apostles, we do not always recognize Jesus until he invites us to table. Think about the last time you were at Mass. How was Jesus present to you in the Scriptures? in the Eucharist? What can you do to recognize Jesus the rest of the week?
- *Do you love me?* Jesus asked Peter this question to give Peter three chances to show his love for the friend he had denied. Is there someone in your life who has hurt you several times, who is hard to forgive over and over? Offer this person up to Jesus in prayer, and ask for help learning how to continue living as a forgiving person.
- *Tend my lambs.* Close your eyes and imagine you are a lamb being held tenderly in the arms of Jesus. After a few minutes, open your eyes and write your feelings in your journal. Do not try to explain them or even to write whole sentences, just record how it felt to be held by Jesus.
- *Follow me.* Jesus invites all of us to be disciples. How do you follow Jesus? Write a prayer asking Jesus to teach you how to follow him more closely in your everyday life.

Activity Ideas

The following activity ideas also relate to the Scripture readings. You may want to read the passage(s) indicated as part of the activity.

- After reading about the Apostles' clash with authorities in the first readings, pose this question to the teens: What would you do if the authorities shut your church today and told you no one could speak about Jesus? If you know someone who has lived in a communist country, invite him or her to give a witness talk to the teens about what religious freedom means to him or her. (Acts 5:27–32,40–41)

- Borrow a button maker and allow the teens to make buttons representing today's psalm. They can draw pictures of life preserver rings with mottoes such as, "Jesus is my lifeguard" or "Jesus rescues me." (Ps. 30:2,4,5–6, 11–12,13)

- Ask the teens to do a dramatic reading of Peter's denial of Jesus, found in the Passion (Luke 22:54–62), and of Peter's confession of love, found in today's Gospel reading. Instead of reading one passage and then the other, read the first denial, then the first expression of love. Next, read the second denial, then the second expression of love. (John 21:1–19)

- In both the second reading and the Gospel, we hear about Jesus as the Lamb of God. Ask the teens to pray the Lamb of God acclamation they are familiar with from Mass. Ask them to discuss the following questions:
  - How does this prayer relate to today's Gospel?
  - What do we mean when we call Jesus the Lamb of God?
  - How does Jesus take away the sins of the world?
  - Why do we need God's mercy?

    After the discussion, ask the teens to pray the acclamation again slowly and reverently. (Rev. 5:11–14; John 21:1–19)

Fourth Sunday of Easter

Scripture Readings (52)
- ❖ Acts 13:14,43–52
- ❖ Ps. 100:1–2,3,5
- ❖ Rev. 7:9,14–17
- ❖ John 10:27–30

God's Word

A major theme of the Scripture readings is "Jesus, our shepherd."

In today's reading from the Acts of the Apostles, Paul and Barnabas continue the work of the Apostles, the mission of Jesus, by traveling from town to town sharing the Good News. The reaction to this Good News is mixed and ranges from enthusiasm to jealousy. While some Jews become followers of Jesus, others react violently and cast the disciples out of their area. The disciples then turn to sharing their message with non-Jews. They are fulfilling Jesus' command to be "a light" to all nations.

Today's psalm and Gospel reading also emphasize the image of Jesus as Lamb of God. And we see Jesus as Shepherd, guiding us who are part of his flock. We are God's people. God looks after us with faithfulness and kindness. We respond to God, our shepherd, with joyful song. All lands are called to join in this song of praise.

The writer of the Book of Revelation sees Jesus as a warrior lamb. Revelation, written at a time of persecution, hopes to give heart to the believers. This Lamb is both redeemer and savior because he will lead a battle against the evil one and bring the holy ones to victory. Here we see some vivid Passover and baptism imagery: "'They have washed their robes and made them white in the blood of the Lamb.'" Those who suffer with Christ are baptized in his blood and will celebrate the Resurrection with Christ.

In the Gospel reading, Jesus, the good shepherd, speaks lovingly of his sheep. Jesus knows each and every one of us by name, and we are to listen to Jesus' voice. When we recognize the voice of Jesus, we must choose whether or not to listen. Sometimes we stray away, yet the Shepherd watches over all the sheep in the flock. God has entrusted the flock to Jesus, so the sheep have nothing to fear. We belong to God. We belong to Jesus. We are safe in the arms of the Shepherd.

Themes for Teens The following themes from the Scriptures relate to the lives of teens:
- The Good News is for all.
- We are God's flock.
- Flock to Jesus.
- Hear the Shepherd's voice.
- The Lamb and the Shepherd are one.

Our Response

Activity ## Where Are the Sheep?

This icebreaker is keyed to the Gospel reading. It is a fun way to start the teens thinking about the role of Jesus as the Shepherd guiding his flock and about Jesus' love for every lamb in the flock.

Play a version of hide-and-seek. If possible, go outside for this activity. Designate one person to be the shepherd and the others the sheep. Tell some of the sheep that they want to be found. Tell the others to do whatever they can to avoid being found. Once the shepherd finds a sheep, this sheep joins the shepherd in searching for the others until all the sheep become shepherds and all the sheep are found.

After the game is over, gather the young people together and share today's Gospel. Ask the teens:
- What did you learn about today's Gospel from the icebreaker?
- Who is the shepherd?
- Who are the sheep?
- How do the sheep get lost?
- How does Jesus find them?

Activity Ideas The following activity ideas also relate to the Scripture readings. You may want to read the passage(s) indicated as part of the activity.

- Paul and Barnabas spread the Good News by traveling on foot from town to town. Today we have many more means of transportation and communication. What are some of the ways we can spread the Good News? Direct each small group of teens to compose a twenty-five-word e-mail message about Jesus. Ask each group to share what it wrote with the other groups. Exchange e-mail addresses with a youth group in another city and share the Good News. (Acts 13:14,43–52)

- In the Gospel Jesus says, "'I know my sheep and mine know me.'" Ask the teens to answer these questions in their journal:
  ○ How does God know me?
  ○ How do I know God?

(John 10:27–30)

- Gather the teens together for prayer. After reading the Gospel, ask the teens to imagine that they are a lamb being held by a shepherd. After a short period of silence, pass a small, stuffed lamb around the group and invite the teens to place their needs in the hands of God. If you can find or fashion a shepherd's staff, pass it around the circle and invite the teens to ask the Good Shepherd to guide them on their journey in life. (Ps. 100:1–2,3,5; Rev. 7:9,14–17; John 10:27–30)

- If the bishop in your diocese lives nearby, arrange for a field trip to visit him. Ask the bishop to show his crosier to the teens and explain what it symbolizes. Invite the young people to ask the bishop about his role as a shepherd of Jesus' flock. If you live in a large diocese geographically, a letter may be more practical. (Ps. 100:1–2,3,5; Rev. 7:9,14–17; John 10:27–30)

Fifth Sunday of Easter

Scripture Readings (55)

- ❖ Acts 14:21–27
- ❖ Ps. 145:8–9,10–11,12–13
- ❖ Rev. 21:1–5
- ❖ John 13:31–33,34–35

God's Word

A major theme of the Scripture readings is "Love one another."

This reading from Acts continues to trace the steps of Paul and Barnabas as they proclaim the Good News. Here we see them returning to some of the places where they had earlier established Christian communities to encourage the believers and help them stay steadfast in faith. They do not tell them that things will be easy, but that faith in Jesus will help them get through the tough times. The disciples also help the young churches choose leaders to stand on their behalf when they have to move on. They return home to their first community to share the exciting news of how much the young church has grown. They do not celebrate their own deeds, but the actions of God working through them.

Psalm 145 is a hymn of both praise and thanksgiving. God is described as gracious, merciful, even-tempered, kind, and compassionate. Through all creation and the works of our own hands, we are to praise God. The second part of the psalm describes God's kingly virtues—mighty and glorious, with an everlasting Kingdom. Our God is both mighty and compassionate. All creatures great and small are called to love and praise our God.

The writer of the Book of Revelation describes a whole new world unlike anything we can imagine. In this totally new creation, good will never be overcome by evil and the new Jerusalem will fulfill all hopes for peace and happiness. God dwells in this new city and makes all things new.

Jesus gives us a new commandment in today's Gospel reading: Love one another. In this leave-taking message, Jesus tells us that being Christian means living in loving relationships with others—like the relationship Jesus has with the Father. People should be able to tell we are Christians by the way we love one another.

This mission of love is not just for Jesus' Apostles but for all of us to live. We look to the life of Jesus to learn how to respect each person and how to live in love with others. Jesus lived this commandment to love every day. As Christians, we proclaim the love of Christ through the way we live in harmony with one another.

Themes for Teens

The following themes from the Scriptures relate to the lives of teens:

- Keep the faith.
- Praise God.
- God creates a new you.
- Christians live love.
- Love one another.

Our Response

Activity

Jesus, Love's Best Teacher

This Scripture study is keyed to the readings as a whole. It gives the young people ideas of how to live Jesus' commandment to love one another, by looking for examples from Jesus' life as depicted in the Scriptures.

Give each small group of teens several red poster board hearts and a Bible. Ask the groups to hunt through the Scriptures for examples of how Jesus lived the commandment, "Love one another." On one side of each heart, have them write the Scripture citation and one sentence describing the passage. On the other side of the heart, ask them to write a suggestion of how we can follow this example in our everyday life.

After the teens share their answer with the entire group, invite them to give the hearts to another youth group, for example, a younger religious education class, so that Jesus' love can continue to spread to others.

Activity Ideas

The following activity ideas also relate to the Scripture readings. You may want to read the passage(s) indicated as part of the activity.

- We, just like the members of the early church, need encouragement from time to time. Ask each teen to trace and cut out an outline of her or his hand. With masking tape, tape the paper handprint onto each teen's back. Ask the teens to give one another a "pat-on-the-back" by writing words of encouragement on one another's handprint. (Acts 14:21–27)

- Explain that to begin something new, we need to let go of the old; if we want to put something in a full closet, we need to give something away. Ask, "Why not do some spring cleaning of your heart?" In their journal, have the teens write down some of the things they need to throw out or clean up. Tell them not to worry about the past; God makes all things new again. (Rev. 21:1–5)

- Ask the teens to bring some hackey sacks to your next meeting or class. If some do not know how to play, allow time for a lesson. The object of the game is to keep the hackey sack from touching the ground by using only your feet and knees. Divide the teens into groups of four. Ask each group to see how many times it can go before the hackey sack touches the ground. If a group keeps it aloft six times, the group members need to think of six different names for God; eight times, eight different names for God; and so on. (Ps. 145:8–9,10–11,12–13)

- Ask the teens, "If a starship landed on your youth group planet tomorrow, how could you tell if there were Christians aboard? What do you need to do in your own group to better live Jesus' commandment of love?" (John 13:31–33)

Sixth Sunday of Easter

God's Word

A major theme of the Scripture readings is "Peace, the gift of the Spirit."

Today's first reading shows us that things were not always idyllic in the early church. Besides persecution from the outside, conflict and tension existed between the Jewish and Gentile Christians. In this case, the church in Antioch is confused about where Mosaic law and Christian practice overlap. They send representatives to the Apostles in Jerusalem for help and advice. The result is a peaceful compromise between Jewish and Gentile Christians. The Apostles are careful not to take the credit. "'"It is the decision of the Holy Spirit, and ours too,"'" they said. The Spirit guided the early church as it grew.

The psalm today asks the entire world and every nation on earth to praise God. The earth's many blessings are God's blessing to us, and we are to remember that we depend on the goodness of God. The first verse is a petition, asking God for blessings and forgiveness. Later, God is called our guide through life. We are asked to show reverence and respect and to approach God with wonder and awe.

The writer of the Book of Revelation views the new city of Jerusalem through the eyes of a jeweler, comparing it to the radiance of a precious gem. The number 12, a symbol of perfection, plays a key role here as the new and old are brought together: 12 tribes of Israel, 12 Apostles, 12 gates, 12 angels, and 12 stones in the foundation. The last part of the reading talks about God as temple. The new Jerusalem does not need a temple, because now God dwells directly among the people. We do not need a church to worship God. God's glory shines through the light of Christ, and we can praise God wherever we are.

In today's Gospel reading, Jesus bids farewell to his disciples and promises to send them the gifts of peace and the Spirit. Jesus speaks again about the closeness of his relationship to the Father. Jesus' words come from the Father, and those who love Jesus love the Father. By promising to send the Holy Spirit, Jesus assures the Apostles that they will not be alone. The Father sends Jesus, who sends the Holy Spirit. The Spirit continues the teaching of Jesus and guides the Apostles in their ministry.

Jesus also gives the peace above all understanding. This is a peace no one can take from us.

Themes for Teens

The following themes from the Scriptures relate to the lives of teens:

- Learn to compromise.
- All the earth praise God.
- Don't keep God in a building.
- God and Jesus and Spirit are one.
- Spirit is the gift of Jesus.

Our Response

Activity   Youth Stand Against Violence

This discussion activity is keyed to the first reading. It helps the teens to share in Jesus' gift of peace by urging them to take a stand against violence.

Invite the teens to take the following self-inventory on violence:

1. What words or actions do you consider violent?
2. What are some examples of violence you have experienced firsthand?
3. Do you believe that violent actions teach others to be violent? How or why?
4. Do you believe that anything positive can come from violence? What? Why?
5. What kinds of negative words come up in your conversations with family and friends?
6. Are you quick to judge without having all the facts? When? Why?
7. Do you ignore the harm that can result from harsh words, teasing sarcasm, and put-downs?
8. Do you let some people know that you really dislike them? What do you say or do to communicate this message?
9. Are you contributing to violence by laughing at or telling jokes that focus on sexism or racism, or that perpetuate stereotypes? What do you do when you hear people tell inappropriate jokes?
10. How do you deal with anger?
11. What skills or habits do you need to practice in order to take a stand against violence?

On a chalkboard or flip chart, write the following six skills or habits that promote peace in human relationships. Ask each person to rank himself or herself in these skills, using the following categories and ranges:

(5 – 1) most to least needed in family
(5 – 1) most to least difficult for me to do
(5 – 1) most frequently to least frequently performed by me

1. *Disagree with style.* Learn to disagree in a calm manner. (needed ___ difficult ___ frequently performed ___)
2. *Be family-friendly.* Begin by greeting your family when you come home. Learn to share and be polite. (needed ___ difficult ___ frequently performed ___)
3. *Say you are sorry.* Recognize that you make mistakes. Be humble enough to offer an apology. (needed ___ difficult ___ frequently performed ___)
4. *Follow directions.* Promote respect of appropriate authority. (needed ___ difficult ___ frequently performed ___)
5. *Take no for an answer.* *No* is an important word to be able to accept. (needed ___ difficult ___ frequently performed ___)
6. *Accept help.* We all need to learn how to ask for and accept help when we need it. (needed ___ difficult ___ frequently performed ___)

Then, in small groups, ask the young people to offer positive suggestions to one another on how to accomplish each person's greatest need.

Close by stressing that each person needs to do his or her part to take a stand against violence and to live Jesus' message of peace.

(Adapted from Everson, "Making a Stand Against Violence")

Easter

Activity Ideas

The following activity ideas also relate to the Scripture readings. You may want to read the passage(s) indicated as part of the activity.

- In the first reading, the Apostles called on the Holy Spirit for help in times of conflict. Their response to the church in Antioch said, """It is the decision of the Holy Spirit, and ours too."" In your journal, write down a decision you need to face right now. List the pros and cons for each choice in the decision. Write a prayer asking the Spirit to help you make the right decision. (Acts 15:1–2,22–29)

- Combine the psalm and Gospel to share the following prayer:
  O Father, let all the nations praise you.
  O Jesus, let all the nations praise you.
  O Spirit, let all the nations praise you.

    (Ps. 67:2–3,5,6,8; John 14:23–29)

- Ask the teens to describe or, if possible, bring in some of their keepsakes and treasures. They can show them to one another and describe the special meaning of each item. Then ask the following questions:
  - What do you give to someone if you want them to remember you? a locket? a picture?
  - Jesus sent the living, breathing Spirit to the Apostles and to us. How does that make you feel?

    (John 14:23–29)

- Here are some icebreakers that go with the responsorial psalm, "O God, let all the nations praise you!"
  1. Cut out newspaper letters to spell out the words in the psalm.
  2. Give the teens 3 minutes to name as many countries as they can whose people praise the Lord.
  3. Give the teens ten names of God in different languages and let them match the word with the language it is written in.

    (Ps. 67:2–3,5,6,8)

Seventh Sunday of Easter

Scripture Readings (62)

- ❖ Acts 7:55–60
- ❖ Ps. 97:1–2,6–7,9
- ❖ Rev. 22:12–14,16–17,20
- ❖ John 17:20–26

God's Word

A major theme of the Scripture readings is "Come, Lord Jesus."

In today's reading from Acts we see a disciple pay the price for what he believes. Stephen sees the glory of God, proclaims what he sees, and dies for his faith. The death of Stephen—the first martyr—marks the beginning of the persecution of the church. The onlookers are so upset by Stephen's words that they drag him out of the city and throw rocks at him until he dies from his injuries. Even as Stephen is being stoned, his faith does not waver. He says,

"'Lord Jesus, receive my spirit.'" Until he dies, his thoughts are of others, and he even asks God to forgive the very people who are killing him.

This psalm praises God as a just king, a king who sits on a throne of justice. At the time the psalms were written, some people still worshiped a group of pagan gods. In Psalm 97, the writer makes it clear that God is *the* God. All the so-called pagan gods are far below the one true God, called Lord of the Most High. In the face of God's power, the other deities are nothing.

This passage from Revelation brings the book to an end. The passage itself begins and ends with the promise that Jesus will return. These are welcome, comforting words for the persecuted Christians. Jesus refers to himself as the Alpha and the Omega, the beginning and the end. Just as God is eternal, Jesus promises to give us the life-giving water of eternal life. Jesus as "root" and "morning star" harks back to the prophets. "Morning star" is a symbol of power. All are urged to repent and be ready when Jesus comes, for each person is sure to get what he or she deserves.

In the Gospel reading, Jesus prays to his Father. He offers a prayer for the disciples and for all people who will come to believe in Jesus through the disciples. Jesus prays that all will come to know the Father through Jesus and that believers all over the world will be open to the Good News.

Jesus' prayer is also a call for unity. Just as God and Jesus are united as one, Jesus unites us to himself and the Father. We are joined together as a community by our faith in God. Our unity with God and Jesus prepares us—like the disciples—for our mission to the world.

Themes for Teens

The following themes from the Scriptures relate to the lives of teens:
- Praise our God and King.
- Come together in Christ.
- Jesus is coming.
- Drink the life-giving water.
- Jesus and God are one.

Our Response

Activity

Yarn Web Prayer

This activity invites the young people to share a prayer inspired by today's Gospel reading and to pray for the unity of all Christians throughout the world.

Purchase or prepare a ball of multicolored yarn for this prayer. Begin the prayer by holding on to the end of the ball of yarn and sharing a prayer inspired by today's Gospel reading, where Jesus prays for the unity of all Christians just as he and the Father are one. Then pass the ball of yarn to another person anywhere in the circle and ask her or him to share a prayer. Continue in this manner, making sure that everyone holds on to their place on the string of yarn as they pass the ball along.

Explain that the yarn's many colors symbolize that though we are very different from one another, we are all one in Jesus Christ. We may have different ways of sharing our faith and practicing our faith, but we are all joined together by our faith in Jesus Christ.

(Adapted from Brown, *Hard Times Catalog for Youth Ministry*, p. 212)

Activity Ideas

The following activity ideas also relate to the Scripture readings. You may want to read the passage(s) indicated as part of the activity.

- In their journal, invite the teens to write a prayer every day this week addressing God by one of the names found in the second reading, for example, Morning Star, Alpha and Omega, Root. (Rev. 22:12–14,16–17,20)

• In the Gospel, Jesus prays for the disciples' mission to the world. In the first reading, we see Stephen pay the price for his mission. Invite someone to talk to your young people about the blessings and the struggles of missionary work. You can invite someone from the United States who has gone to another country, or you may want to give the teens a chance to hear from someone who came from another country to do mission work here in the United States. Make sure you allow time for the teens to ask questions. (Acts 7:55–60; John 17:20–26)

  • In the second reading, we hear about the life-giving water of eternal life. Send the teens to the Scriptures to find another place where Jesus teaches about life-giving water. If they get stumped, invite them to read John 4:5–26, about the woman at the well. Ask the teens to put themselves in the shoes of the woman. How did she react to the promise of life-giving water? (Rev. 22: 2–14,16–17,20)

 • Invite young people from another Christian church to join your teens for a youth group meeting, or visit a youth group at another church. Make sure the activities you plan share common ground, but do not make the other group uncomfortable. With the permission of parents, join the teens from the other church for one of their services, and then invite them to attend Mass with you. Later, ask the teens to identify some of the things both groups have in common. Include a prayer for Christian unity as part of this bridge-building experience. (John 17:20–26)

Pentecost Sunday

Scripture Readings (64)

❖ Acts 2:1–11
❖ Ps. 104:1,24,29–30,31,34
❖ 1 Cor. 12:3–7,12–13
❖ John 20:19–23

God's Word

A major theme of the Scripture readings is "One in the Holy Spirit."

All of today's readings speak about the Spirit of Jesus gifting his disciples with the talents and powers for going forth with courage to proclaim the Good News.

The first reading, from Acts, describes the events of Pentecost, in which the Holy Spirit comes upon the Apostles in wind and fire. When they are filled with the Holy Spirit, they begin to speak in languages they never knew before. The assembled crowd is astonished. Though many of the crowd are foreigners, they understand that the disciples are speaking about the wonders of God. God has reversed the Tower of Babel. Rather than being confused by the different languages, the people can understand them.

Psalm 104 is a hymn of praise to God, who sends forth the Spirit to renew the face of the whole earth.

The second reading is a reminder that the Spirit bestows gifts for proclaiming the Good News on everyone, but not everyone has the same kinds of gifts. The gifts of the Spirit are public gifts, not private ones. And when people use them to complement the gifts of others, the community forms the one Body of Christ in which the Spirit is alive.

The early Christians probably argued about whose gifts were the most important. As one Body in Christ, divisions such as race, age, or nationality lose all meaning. The image of the body was chosen to highlight that the community is not a static, unmoving group. A living body grows and moves and changes; so, too, does the church community if it is to stay alive.

Today's reading from the Gospel of John is Jesus' promise of the Holy Spirit. The disciples are hiding out, scared and defeated. Jesus comes to them and breathes new life into them—the breath of the Spirit. With the gift of the Spirit comes the gift of peace and a mandate to go out and forgive the sins of others.

Themes for Teens

The following themes from the Scriptures relate to the lives of teens:
- Be filled with the Holy Spirit.
- Lord, send us your Spirit.
- Our gifts are to serve.
- We are the Body of Christ.
- The Spirit offers us peace.

Our Response

Activity

Filled with the Spirit

This activity, keyed to the readings as a whole, asks the teens to reflect on the power of the Holy Spirit to change the lives of the disciples and to change our lives. It invites the teens to reflect on what it means to be filled with the Holy Spirit.

Give each of the teens an uninflated balloon. Ask them to describe the balloon—small, flat, lifeless, and so forth. Allow them time to blow the balloon up. Ask them to describe the balloon now—how it is different.

The Spirit blows new life into us, breathes new life into us. Talk about what the disciples were like before the Spirit came to them and what they were like after they were filled with the Holy Spirit.

Ask: "How does the Holy Spirit change and empower us? What happens when we are filled with the Holy Spirit?" Attach one of the gifts of the Holy Spirit—wisdom, understanding, courage, knowledge, right judgment, reverence, wonder, and awe—to each balloon. Direct the teens to form groups based on the gift that is attached to their balloon. Ask each group to discuss and share its answer to the question, "How does this gift of the Holy Spirit enable us to better live our faith in our everyday life?"

Activity Ideas

The following activity ideas also relate to the Scripture readings. You may want to read the passage(s) indicated as part of the activity.

- In the first reading, the Spirit inspires the disciples to speak in many languages so that everyone will be able to hear the Good News in their own language. Challenge the teens to do some translating of today's psalm, "Lord, send out your Spirit." Give them a week to learn how to say and write this psalm refrain in another language. Next week, Trinity Sunday, give the teens some time to teach one another how to pray this refrain in each language. See how many different languages the teens can use to pray this refrain. (Acts 2:1–11)

- In the Gospel, "[Jesus] breathed on [the disciples] and said: 'Receive the Holy Spirit.'" The Holy Spirit has been called the breath of God, and it is described in the form of wind as well as of fire. Ask the teens to fill out and share their responses to this icebreaker at the start of your meeting on the Holy Spirit.

  Are you:
  ○ out of breath
  ○ catching your breath
  ○ like a breath of fresh air
  ○ a breath saver
  ○ short on breath
  ○ seeing your breath on a cold day
  ○ other _____

  (Acts 2:1–11; John 20:19–23)

- This Gospel passage is often cited as the time when Jesus conferred the power to forgive sins in the sacrament of reconciliation. Invite a priest to talk about what it means to have Jesus act through him in the sacrament of reconciliation. Or ask someone who has seen the sacrament change through the years to compare what it was like to go anonymously into the confessional box and what it is like today to have the option of a face-to-face conversation. (John 20:19–23)

- In the second reading, we hear how each person is given gifts by the Spirit to share for the good of the Christian community. Invite the teens to help sponsor a ministry fair for your parish or school. It can be a great way to make people aware of the different ways to minister in the church community. The young people can help advertise the event, set up the tables and booths, and serve refreshments. Teens and parishioners can be encouraged to volunteer their time and share their gifts in different ministries. (1 Cor. 12:3–7,12–13)

Trinity Sunday

Scripture Readings (167)
❖ Prov. 8:22–31
❖ Ps. 8:4–5,6–7,8–9
❖ Rom. 5:1–5
❖ John 16:12–15

God's Word A major theme of the Scripture readings is "The spirit of truth."

This reading from Proverbs describes Wisdom as a playful companion of the Creator who was with God from the beginning. Wisdom existed before the seas or the mountains were made. Wisdom also helped in the creation of the world and rejoiced and delighted in the creation of people. The character of Wisdom here may also anticipate the coming of Jesus, the firstborn of God, who also existed before creation and was God's agent in the creation of humankind. How exciting and amazing to imagine Jesus and the Creator taking delight in the creation of each one of us.

This psalm can be a response to the Creation story found in Proverbs. The author contrasts the power of God with the frailty of human beings, and marvels that God takes time out from such a busy schedule to give us even a passing glance. God values each of us so much that we have a place close to the angels. The world we live in is a gift from the Creator to be cherished by humankind.

In Paul's Letter to the Romans, Jesus is called the source of all peace. We find our way to God through Jesus. Our afflictions teach us endurance, which teaches us hope. Because of Jesus we can hope that God will deliver us from our troubles. God's love was born in Jesus and continues in the Holy Spirit.

Today's reading from the Gospel of John helps us understand the role of the Holy Spirit. The disciples felt lost at the thought that Jesus was leaving them. Jesus, in saying farewell to these friends, promises to send the Spirit of truth to continue teaching and guiding them. It is not until after the Resurrection that the disciples will begin to understand Jesus' message. They will need the Spirit to help them understand what Jesus was really all about. The Spirit continues the bond between God the Father, Jesus, and the People of God.

Themes for Teens The following themes from the Scriptures relate to the lives of teens:
- God delights in us.
- Praise God's name.
- God loves us through the Spirit.
- The Spirit is our guide.
- Father, Son, and Spirit are one.

Our Response

Activity **In Perfect Harmony**

This exercise is keyed to the Gospel reading. It uses the harmony of music to offer a glimpse at the mystery of the Trinity—three persons in one God.

Invite a musician to play a familiar church song for the teens. The song must have three parts of harmony. Divide the teens into three groups. Teach one part of the harmony to each group. Once the teens have practiced it a few times and feel confident they can hold their own, put all the parts together in song.

Ask the teens if they can still hear each part of the harmony when they sing all three together. Yet note that it becomes one song when sung all together.

Ask the young people to compare this exercise to what they know about the Trinity. The Father, the Son, and the Holy Spirit are each separate, yet they are one in God.

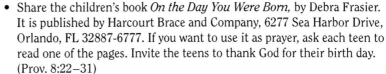

Activity Ideas The following activity ideas also relate to the Scripture readings. You may want to read the passage(s) indicated as part of the activity.

- After sharing the first reading, urge the teens to go home and ask their parents about the day they were born. Invite them to imagine their "birth day" and themselves as an image of God's delight. (Prov. 8:22–31)

- Share the children's book *On the Day You Were Born*, by Debra Frasier. It is published by Harcourt Brace and Company, 6277 Sea Harbor Drive, Orlando, FL 32887-6777. If you want to use it as prayer, ask each teen to read one of the pages. Invite the teens to thank God for their birth day. (Prov. 8:22–31)

- Offer prayers for the teens who are graduating at this time of the year. Ask the Holy Spirit to strengthen and guide them as they leave their high school or parish for a new community. (All readings)

Corpus Christi Sunday

Scripture Readings (169)
- ❖ Gen. 14:18–20
- ❖ Ps. 110:1,2,3,4
- ❖ 1 Cor. 11:23–26
- ❖ Luke 9:11–17

God's Word

A major theme of the Scripture readings is "Bread, blessed and broken."

In this reading from Genesis, Melchizedek, the king of Salem, brings bread and wine to celebrate Abraham's victory over his enemies. He offers a prayer of praise to God, because God had delivered Abraham's enemies into his hands. Melchizedek, who is also a priest, blesses Abraham. It is easy to attach eucharistic meaning to this passage from the first book of the Bible because bread is offered. In the Christian Testament, Jesus is called the high priest according to the order of Melchizedek.

This psalm, written for a king on coronation day, can also be easily read to point to Jesus. The Lord sits at the right hand of God, and all enemies become his footstool. This psalm is mentioned often in the Hebrew Scriptures.

Only a few disciples sat at the table with Jesus at the Last Supper, when Jesus gave us his body and blood in the first celebration of the Eucharist. After sharing his body in the form of bread, and his blood in the form of wine, Jesus tells the disciples, "'Do this in remembrance of me.'" The Eucharist is a tradition to be handed on, to be received and shared. It is a living remembrance of Jesus' sacrifice of love.

Jesus spent a long day healing the sick and preaching to a large group of followers. It was getting late, and perhaps even the disciples' stomachs were growling. The disciples told Jesus to send everyone home for dinner. Instead, Jesus told them to make dinner. All they could scrounge up were five loaves of bread and two fish. Surely Jesus would change his mind. But Jesus told them to organize everyone into groups and get them seated. Jesus prayed over the loaves and fish and asked the disciples to start handing out the food. What they probably thought would be quick work took awhile, and the food kept coming and coming. Imagine their surprise when everyone had eaten their fill and there were still lots of leftovers. In this miracle, the only one found in all four Gospels, Jesus not only feeds the people but teaches the disciples how to minister to others. Jesus' blessing of the bread also mirrors the Eucharist. We are a eucharistic community. We share the Body of Christ in the Eucharist, but we are also called to feed others in the Body of Christ.

Themes for Teens

The following themes from the Scriptures relate to the lives of teens:
- Bread is blessed and broken.
- Praise God, our blessing.
- Do this and remember me.
- We are the Body of Christ.

Our Response

Activity   Table Prayers

This activity is keyed to all the readings. The prayers invite the teens to reflect on the connection between God's blessing of food for our body and the gift of the Eucharist as food for our soul.

Ask the teens if they know any prayers or graces to say before meals. Pray them together.

Here are two popular ones:

Bless us, O Lord,
And these your gifts,
Which we are about to receive
From your bounty,
Through Christ, our Lord.
Amen.

God is great; God is good.
Let us thank him for our food.
Amen.

Invite the teens each to write two prayers—one, a prayer to pray before meals with their family; and the second, a prayer or blessing to say before receiving Communion.

Compile and publish the prayers of the teens in a booklet. Make several copies—one for each of them to take home and use with their family at the dinner table each night; and others to share with parishioners in your parish or students at your school.

Activity Ideas   The following activity ideas also relate to the Scripture readings. You may want to read the passage(s) indicated as part of the activity.

- Ask the teens the following questions:
  - How many times a day do you eat?
  - How many days a week do you eat?
  - What happens when you go too long without eating?
  - How often do you receive Jesus in the Eucharist?
  - Is it enough to feed ourselves spiritually only once a week?
  - What happens when we go too long without nourishment for the soul?
    (1 Cor. 11:23–26; Luke 9:11–17)

- Ask someone from your parish or school who attends daily Mass to talk about why it is important to them. Invite the teens to attend daily Mass as a group for one week. (1 Cor. 11:23–26)

- After sharing the Gospel together, ask the teens to reflect quietly on this question: "How can you be the Body of Christ for others?" (Luke 9:11–17)

- Teach the teens one of these songs: "I Am the Living Bread," "Table Song," "The Living Bread of God," or "Here in This Place," some wonderful songs from the album *Table Songs,* by David Haas (Chicago: GIA Pulbications, 1991). (1 Cor. 11:23–26; Luke 9:11–17)

Easter

Ordinary Time

Second Sunday of the Year

Scripture Readings (67)

- ❖ Isa. 62:1–5
- ❖ Ps. 96:1–2,2–3,7–8,9–10
- ❖ 1 Cor. 12:4–11
- ❖ John 2:1–12

God's Word

A major theme of the Scripture readings is "The transforming power of God's love."

In Isaiah we learn how we are seen in the eyes of God as the most precious of gifts—valuable as a glorious crown, called "'My Delight,'" and as beloved as a bride in the eyes of a groom. Even more than a couple who commit themselves to each other for life, God's commitment to us is unwavering and everlasting. No matter how others may put us down, no matter how our own self-doubts and failings bring us down, nothing can diminish us in the sight of God.

The psalm calls us to praise the many wonderful things God has done for us. To praise God, we must first take stock of the gifts given to us. This psalm also asks us to make this praise a community ritual and to join with the community to worship our God. God's word is not to be kept to ourselves; we are called to proclaim it to others.

In Paul's First Letter to the Corinthians, we hear how we are uniquely gifted by God and about the different ways the Spirit calls us to minister with these gifts. No one gift or ministry is more important than another. Paul warns those in Corinth that God's gifts should not be a source of competition but rather an occasion to serve others.

This excerpt from John's Gospel is the first of many signs chronicled by the author. It is often highlighted as an example of how Jesus listened to his mother, doing what she requested even though his "'hour [had] not yet come.'" However, in John's Gospel, it is also one of the first events in Jesus' public ministry. This miracle is not a great, noisy spectacle. Jesus does not detract from the bride and groom as the center of attention. Yet he does something astounding—changes water into wine—and gives us a hint of the power of God to transform our life. We see God's glory manifested in Jesus, and we begin our reflection on who Jesus is and how he will change our life. This reading also foreshadows Jesus' death. When his hour comes, it will be the hour of his death.

Key in all these readings is commitment—God's commitment to us, our commitment to ministry, a marriage commitment, and Jesus' commitment to change our life for the better.

Themes for Teens

The following themes from the Scriptures relate to the lives of teens:
- We shine in the eyes of God.
- Share your gifts.
- Jesus transforms us.
- You are a gift.
- Be open to change.
- God's love is expressed in the gifts and talents we possess.

Ordinary Time

Our Response

Activity

Naming Our Gifts

This affirmation activity encourages the young people to reflect on their gifts and the gifts of others in light of the second reading. It challenges them to identify ways they can minister to others. This activity works best with teens who have known one another for some time.

Give each teen a marker and a piece of 10½-by-14-inch white, heavy-stock paper or poster board. Ask the young people to use large block letters to spell their name, filling up the entire paper. Instruct them to leave the inside of the letters blank so that there is plenty of room to write inside. Hang the name posters around the meeting space so that they are all visible and reachable.

Ask the young people to identify the gifts and talents they see in one another. Urge them to stay away from superficial comments such as, "nice smile" or "cool clothes," and to concentrate on qualities such as, "good listener," "always willing to help," or "good at speaking in front of others." Give them 10 to 15 minutes to move around the room and write gifts and talents on one another's name cards. Ask them to try to identify a quality for each person before writing several on any one card.

Next, read First Corinthians 12:4–11.

Allow the teens to take their name cards down from the wall and read what others have written about them. Ask the teens to look at their gifts in light of the reading and to identify at least one way they might use their gifts to serve others—at home, at school, at work, or in the parish community. In groups of six to eight teens, invite them to share these possibilities.

Close by encouraging them to continue or to start a new ministry using the gifts they talked about during this session.

Note: If the teens are unfamiliar with one another, you may want to do a self-affirmation as an alternate activity. You can ask the young people to identify some of their own gifts and talents before identifying ways they can share them with others.

Activity Ideas

The following activity ideas also relate to the Scripture readings. You may want to read the passage(s) indicated as part of the activity.

- Invite parishioners to explain how they share their gifts through parish ministry. Visible ministries should be represented, such as lectoring and singing in the choir, as well as behind-the-scenes ministries, such as stuffing envelopes, cutting grass, and caring for altar linens. Ask the teens which ministries they would like to help with now, and which ones they hope to do in the future, for example, becoming a eucharistic minister. (1 Cor. 12:4–11)

- Explain that during Sunday liturgy, one of the ways we praise God for gifts received is when we pray "Glory to God in the highest" during the Gloria. Ask how this prayer is like today's psalm, a hymn of praise. Note that we rarely pray this prayer outside of Mass. After a brief discussion, you may want to pray the Gloria together to end your meeting. If your community is accustomed to singing the Gloria—and your group of teens enjoys singing—you may also want to sing it together. (Ps. 96:1–2,2–3,7–8,9–10)

- Explain that today's Gospel tells of one of the first miracles of Jesus' public ministry, in which he changed those around him. Challenge the teens to remember and share some of Jesus' other miracles. Then send them to the Scriptures to find examples of other miracles. (John 2:1–12)

- Invite the teens to reflect in their journal on the following: "At the wedding feast, Jesus changed water into wine. What do you hope Jesus will help you change in your life and in the world around you?" (John 2:1–12)

Third Sunday of the Year

Scripture Readings
(70)

- ❖ Neh. 8:2–4,5–6,8–10
- ❖ Ps. 19:8,9,10,15
- ❖ 1 Cor. 12:12–30
- ❖ Luke 1:1–4; 4:14–21

God's Word

A major theme of the Scripture readings is "Living the word."

Today's reading from the Book of Nehemiah shows reverence for the word of God. The actions of Ezra and the people are similar to the way we approach the Gospel reading at Mass. We may not weep or fall to the ground, but the word of God requires a response. The word of God is for all to see and understand. We are invited to celebrate God's word, take it to heart, and live it.

The psalmist continues the theme of celebrating the word of God as "spirit and life." God's word offers us wisdom and guidelines to live by—not words that "go in one ear and out the other." Here, the law found in this word is not a burden but an expression of God's love.

The second reading uses the image of the body with its many parts to help us understand that each of us is a vital part of the Body of Christ—the church. This continues the theme from last week's second reading that every gift or ministry is as important as the others, every part of the Body of Christ is as valuable as the others. This reading is a call for unity in a divided early church. The Spirit holds the Body together.

In today's Gospel reading, the writer of Luke explains the purpose of his Gospel. In his introduction, we learn that this is not a biography of Jesus and that it must be read through the eyes of faith. Later he records a scene in which Jesus reads from the Scriptures and explains why he has come—not for the rich or the free or the healthy, but to free captives, cheer the poor, and give sight to the blind. Jesus is the fulfillment of the Scriptures. He lives out the Scriptures in day-to-day ministry. When these Scriptures are read, they are directed to us. As Jesus' Body, we are to live out his word by meeting the needs of the deprived, the hurting, and the hungry.

Themes for Teens

The following themes from the Scriptures relate to the lives of teens:
- We are the Body of Christ.
- Jesus is the Word.
- Put the word into action.
- Live the word of God.
- Listen to, celebrate, and proclaim the word.

Our Response

Activity

Listen, Celebrate, and Proclaim

This activity is keyed to the Gospel reading. In this discussion the teens are urged to pay more attention to the Gospel each time they hear it and to discover ways to enjoy it and live it in their everyday life.

Give each teen a sheet of paper and a pencil. During the first part of this activity, the teens may not talk to one another and may only write. They will have 3 minutes to complete the activity. Ask them to write down anything they remember from the readings proclaimed at last Sunday's liturgy.

Note: Avoid asking the teens to share their responses out loud because some of them may have skipped Mass the previous week or may not remember the readings and could be embarrassed.

Share with the young people the idea that the Gospel requires a response from us. One way to approach the Gospel is to listen to, celebrate, and proclaim it.

Divide the teens into three groups and give each group a separate place to work. Have one group brainstorm ways we can be better listeners to the Gospel; have the second group find some ways to celebrate the Gospel; and have the third group list ways to proclaim or share the Gospel. Each group may choose its own way to present its conclusions—using a poster, skit, story, or some other method. Encourage the teens to use their imagination and to be creative. Allow 45 to 60 minutes for the groups to work, and then ask them to return to the large group for the presentations.

Activity Ideas   The following activity ideas also relate to the Scripture readings. You may want to read the passage(s) indicated as part of the activity.

- Before the Gospel is proclaimed, the priest says, "A reading from the Gospel according to Luke." We say "Praise to you Lord, Jesus Christ." Ask the teens what sign they make when saying this. Then ask: "What does it mean when we make the sign of the cross on our forehead, our lips, and our heart? What can we do to better understand the Gospel, proclaim the Gospel, and keep it in our heart?" (Luke 1:1–4; 4:14–21)

- Contact the director of liturgy at your parish and invite her or him to do an abbreviated lector workshop for the teens. Include an explanation of how the lectionary is organized and the order of the readings. If possible, give the teens an opportunity to practice proclaiming the word and critique them so that they can improve their skills. (All readings)

- Make a life-size poster on large butcher paper and trace the outline of a person on it. You can do this easily by having the tallest member of your group lie down on the paper and trace around her or him with a marker. Read today's second reading and write, "We are all part of the Body of Christ" in large letters on the poster. Ask the teens to list with colorful markers inside the outline of the person all the many ministries of service at your parish or school. Hang the poster in a place where all in the community will be able to see it. (1 Cor. 12:17–30)

- Who are some champions of the poor and oppressed in our everyday world? Ask the teens to scour magazines and newspapers to find examples of people who bring "glad tidings to the poor," "liberty to captives," "sight to the blind," or "release to prisoners." (Luke 1:1–4; 4:14–21)

- Have several teens role-play the different parts of the body by engaging in a conversation about how they need one another. (1 Cor. 12:17–30)

Fourth Sunday of the Year

Scripture Readings (73)

- ❖ Jer. 1:4–5,17–19
- ❖ Ps. 71:1–2,3–4,5–6,15–17
- ❖ 1 Cor. 12:31—13:13
- ❖ Luke 4:21–30

God's Word

A major theme of the Scripture readings is "Proclaiming God's word can mean rejection."

The reading from Jeremiah tells the story of Jeremiah's call to be a prophet. When we read it, it helps us recognize that we also have a similar call and, likewise, an intimate relationship with God. Because we have such a close relationship with God, we are told not to fear those who might want to crush us when we proclaim God's word, for "I am with you to deliver you, says the Lord."

The psalmist calls God "rock of refuge, . . . my hope, . . . my trust." This song of praise continues the theme of protection found in the first reading. From the womb to our youth to our old age, God is with us. No matter who we are or what we do, God is there for us. These words could be ours as well as Jeremiah's. When we face serious opposition to who we are and what we stand for, we can look to God for strength.

This week's beautiful reading from First Corinthians celebrates love as the ideal gift from God and the gift we should strive for beyond all others. When we hear this litany of adjectives describing love, it may seem unattainable in light of our human failings, yet we are told love never fails. This reading is probably one of the best known of the readings attributed to Paul. Love should be at the heart of each person's ministry. Love enhances all other gifts. Even the grandest of gifts—prophecy, knowledge, and the like—are nothing without love.

In today's Gospel reading, Jesus did not get a warm reception when he went home to teach. Far from it. When Jesus suggested that the people his audience regarded as nonbelievers were more faithful then those in his audience, they kicked him out of the synagogue. They put him down as just a son of Joseph, the carpenter. Who was he to have the nerve to claim the Scriptures were proclaimed through him?

This would not be the last time Jesus is rejected. Opposition to the word he proclaimed would eventually lead to death. But we need not despair. We can also see this reading as the beginning of our journey toward Easter.

Themes for Teens

The following themes from the Scriptures relate to the lives of teens:
- Love is the greatest gift.
- Being a prophet is not easy.
- Only love lasts.
- God is our rock.
- Even Jesus got rejected.

Ordinary Time

Our Response

Activity **Even Jesus Was Left Out of the Crowd**

This activity is keyed to the Gospel reading. Through drama and discussion, it shows the teens that they are not alone when they are rejected by others—even Jesus was not always welcome. It also encourages them to find ways to be more welcoming and inclusive toward others.

Divide the teens into groups of six to eight. Ask them to think of an example of how teens form cliques to exclude other teens, or of an example of one teen making another teen feel rejected. Each group should prepare a 3-to-5-minute role-play of the situation to present to the large group.

Then read Luke 4:21–30, and use these questions for discussion:

- Describe a time when you felt rejected by others.
- How do you feel when you are rejected?
- What are some ways we reject others or leave others out?
- Why do we treat others this way?
- Why did people reject Jesus?
- How did Jesus respond to rejection?
- What can we learn from Jesus on how to include others?

Activity Ideas The following activity ideas also relate to the Scripture readings. You may want to read the passage(s) indicated as part of the activity.

- Ask the teens to bring in some CDs or cassette tapes of popular love songs. Play part of at least seven or eight of them. Ask one of the teens to read the second reading. Discuss how the messages about love in the songs differ from the description of love in this reading. (1 Cor. 12:31—13:13)

- In the first reading, God says to us also: "'I formed you . . . I knew you . . . I dedicated you.'" Invite the teens, when they are home alone or in their own private prayer space, to close their eyes for a few minutes and repeat these words over and over as a mantra, reflecting on God's great love for them. (Jer. 1:4–5,17–19)

- On the top of a piece of poster board, write the phrase "Love is . . ." Ask the teens to brainstorm words and phrases to complete the sentence. Write these on the left side of the poster. After reading First Corinthians, invite the teens to write on the right side of the poster words and phrases from the reading to complete the sentence. How do we need to change our original list based on what we read in the second reading? (1 Cor. 12:31—13:13)

- Find a copy of a basic recipe for chocolate cake. Rewrite the recipe, leaving out one of the key ingredients—either the flour or the chocolate. Give the teens each a copy of the recipe and ask if they would like to make and eat this cake. When the missing ingredient is noticed, ask what happens when you leave an important ingredient out of a recipe. Read the first half of the second reading. Ask, "What happens when love is the missing ingredient in your relationships with others?" (1 Cor. 12:31—13:13)

Fifth Sunday of the Year

Scripture Readings (76)

- ❖ Isa. 6:1–2,3–8
- ❖ Ps. 138:1–2,2–3,4–5,7–8
- ❖ 1 Cor. 15:1–11
- ❖ Luke 5:1–11

God's Word

A major theme of the Scripture readings is "The invitation to discipleship."

The first reading today leads to the call of the prophet Isaiah. The soon-to-be prophet meets God face-to-face. There are plenty of special effects—angels singing, doors shaking, and smoke. No wonder Isaiah is afraid. He quickly takes stock of his failings and decides he is doomed. But terror turns into an invitation because God bridges the gap from sin to holiness. After an angel touches Isaiah and removes all sin, God asks, "'"Whom shall I send?"'" Isaiah quickly answers, "'Here I am. . . . Send me.'"

The psalmist shows great confidence in God and sings many praises for God's kindness in answering prayers and giving strength. There are many ways to praise God—with song, words, and worship, and by calling on others to praise God.

The second reading is a recap of the beliefs of the early Christians. The author wants listeners to understand the Gospel that saves them. As the Scriptures foretold, Jesus died, was buried, and rose from the dead. A partial list of witnesses—including the author—testifies to this truth. The Corinthians have a tough time grasping what the Resurrection of Jesus means for them. The author reaffirms that the heart of the Gospel is Jesus' death and Resurrection.

Today's reading from Luke's Gospel relates Jesus' preaching and teaching from a boat. When Jesus wants to go fishing, Simon tries to talk him out of it after having caught little during the day. Simon is in for a surprise when the nets come back full of fish. Jesus calls disciples from every way and walk of life, with the particular gifts and skills that we might also have, even though we might not think our gifts and skills are so great.

This imagery of fishing with Jesus is a great way to understand discipleship. Just as fishing without Jesus results in empty nets, trying to live and work without being a disciple of Jesus leaves us empty.

Themes for Teens

The following themes from the Scriptures relate to the lives of teens:

- Send me, God.
- Praise God any way you can.
- Jesus is the heart of the Gospel.
- Catch the message of Jesus.
- Let Jesus catch you in his net.

Our Response

Activity — Fishers of Jesus

This icebreaker is keyed to the first reading. It uses a familiar children's card game to encourage the teens to start thinking about ways they can follow Jesus.

Give a deck of cards to each small group of teens and teach them how to play this variation of the game Go Fish. All the cards are placed face down in the center of the table and scrambled thoroughly. Taking turns, each teen is allowed to turn two cards face up. If they do not match, the cards must be turned over again. If they match, the teen may keep the cards after identifying one way we can be disciples of Jesus—at home, at school, at work, with friends, or in our parish community.

The game is over when all the cards are matched and each group has identified twenty-six ways to follow Jesus. If time permits, each group could share its list with the larger group.

Activity Ideas

The following activity ideas also relate to the Scripture readings. You may want to read the passage(s) indicated as part of the activity.

- We may not see any smoke or hear any angels singing from on high, as Isaiah saw and heard, but God is calling us, too. In their journal, ask the teens to answer this question: "How is God calling you—through nature? other people? quiet time?" (Isa. 6:1–2,3–8)

- After reading this passage from Isaiah, ask the teens to identify a prayer we say at Mass that is similar to the prayer offered by Isaiah to God. Ask them why we pray the Holy, Holy. Invite the teens to pray it slowly, thinking about the words more carefully than they do when rushing through it at Mass on Sunday. (Isa. 6:1–2,3–8)

- Buy several packs of standard party invitations. Fill one out for each teen, written as though it is from Jesus, inviting them to discipleship. Give the invitations out at the end of today's meeting as a reflection to take home. The teens may want to glue the invitation in their prayer journal. (Luke 5:1–11)

- Spread a large fishing net out in the middle of your prayer space and fill it with all types of fishing gear and objects found in and near the sea. Have each teen select an item from the net and offer a prayer of discipleship inspired by the object. (Luke 5:1–11)

Sixth Sunday of the Year

Scripture Readings (79)

- ❖ Jer. 17:5–8
- ❖ Ps. 1:1–2,3,4,6
- ❖ 1 Cor. 15:12,16–20
- ❖ Luke 6:17,20–26

God's Word

A major theme of the Scripture readings is "The challenge of discipleship."

Jeremiah warns that we must place our trust in God rather than in the things of this earth. The prophet is not saying that we should not trust others, only that things of this world are temporary, and we need to look instead to God, who is everlasting. The prophet contrasts a barren bush in the desert with a lush tree planted close to the water, where its roots can reach the stream. We want to be like this tree, reaching out our roots to drink from God's everlasting waters.

The psalmist agrees with Jeremiah and even uses the same example of a tree growing near running water. To be happy, we must avoid wickedness and not keep company with sinners. We must hope in the Lord if we are to bear fruit. Once again we see the contrast between good and evil. Only this time, instead of a barren bush, the wicked are described as chaff flying in the wind.

The reading from Paul's First Letter to the Corinthians targets those in the early church who begin to doubt what kind of resurrection they will experience. This letter is the author's tough response. The early Christians knew bodies could not be raised; they thought they were smarter than that. But if we only believe in what we see and know—that "the dead are not raised"—then we cannot embrace the teaching about the Resurrection of Jesus, either. Jesus' Resurrection and its meaning for us is the center of our faith. We are told not to fall asleep, to stay awake to the hope of Christ resurrected.

The reading from the Gospel of Luke also offers a contrast, but instead of dry land versus water, Jesus offers a contrast between those people who are blessed and those who face great woe. These blessings and woes may seem hard to swallow. We do not view poverty, hunger, and weeping as blessings, and we do all we can to avoid insults and hate.

Once again, Jesus stands on its end the accepted way of looking at things. In Jesus' picture of the Reign of God, the social order is reversed. Those who have much lose much of what they have, and those who have little gain much. This picture of God's Reign will not be readily accepted by those who have much. Choosing to follow Jesus is not always going to be comfortable. It may mean facing hardship.

Themes for Teens

The following themes from the Scriptures relate to the lives of teens:
- Trust in God, not things.
- Place your roots in God.
- The Risen Lord is the center of our faith.
- Following Jesus is a challenge.
- Blessings can come from hardship.

Our Response

Activity

Refreshed by Jesus

This shared prayer uses the vivid imagery of water found in the first reading and the psalm as a call to Jesus to help us through the dry spells in our life.

You will need a Bible, a copy of the responsorial psalm for all to read, a large bowl of water, and a towel. If you are in an outdoor setting for your program or retreat, using a natural source of water would be ideal.
- *Call to prayer.*
- *First reading.* Jer. 17:5–8
- *Responsorial psalm.* Ps. 1:1–2,3,4,6: Have the group read alternate verses, left side and right side.
- *Quiet reflection.* Ask this question: "What is one area in your life where you need Jesus' life-giving water and refreshment?"
- *Shared prayer.* Instruct each teen to offer a prayer asking Jesus' blessing for a dry part of his or her life. As the teens do so, they may come forward and dip their hands in the water, make the sign of the cross with water on their forehead, splash or sprinkle it, or run it through their fingers.

Activity Ideas   The following activity ideas also relate to the Scripture readings. You may want to read the passage(s) indicated as part of the activity.

- Assign the teens some research on the life of Mother Teresa. After their mini-reports, ask: "How was Mother Teresa able to find blessings in the midst of the poverty all around her in India? How does what you have learned from her life help you understand the Gospel passage, "'Blest are you poor; the reign of God is yours.'"" (Luke 6:17,20–26)

- Place a large rock and a big, soaking-wet sponge in the middle of your discussion circle. Ask the teens to complete one of the following two sentences:
  ○ I would rather be a rock because . . .
  ○ I would rather be a sponge because . . .
      Use this reflection as a springboard to understanding the contrasts found in today's readings. (All readings)

- Use this forced-choice icebreaker to engage the young people in the rich imagery and contrasts found in these readings. At the start of your session, give each teen a sheet with at least ten forced-choice questions. Some examples:
      I'd rather be:
      ○ a dry field or a bubbling brook?
      ○ a raging river or a majestic mountain?
      ○ a glass of water or a tray of ice cubes?
      ○ a sandbox or a swimming pool?
      Ask the teens to share with a partner their answers and the reason for making each choice. (All readings)

- Ask each teen to pull a one-dollar bill (or larger) out of her or his pocket and study it. Read Jer. 17:5–8. Challenge the teens to find the message on the one-dollar bill that is also found in Jeremiah. What does it mean when we say, "In God we trust"? (Jer. 17:5–8)

Seventh Sunday of the Year

Scripture Readings (82)
- ❖ 1 Sam. 26:2,7–9,12–13,22–23
- ❖ Ps. 103:1–2,3–4,8,10,12–13
- ❖ 1 Cor. 15:45–49
- ❖ Luke 6:27–38

God's Word   A major theme of the Scripture readings is "Called to compassion."

In the reading from the First Book of Samuel, David has Saul right where he wants him—asleep and vulnerable to attack. But David spares Saul's life because David's respect for God's anointed is stronger than his need for revenge. Even though others egg him on, David spares Saul's life. Taking a jug and a spear, so that the king will know about his close call, David slips away. In David's perspective, it is God's prerogative to punish Saul, not his.

The psalm celebrates God as a God of compassion. God does not seek revenge or punishment of our sins, but forgives, heals, and redeems us.

In his First Letter to the Corinthians, Paul compares and contrasts our human self—patterned after Adam and prone to death, with our spiritual self—patterned after Jesus, the Second Adam, and prone to life.

In the Gospel reading, Jesus calls us to show a Godlike compassion by forgiving our enemies. This is tough in an age when revenge is a lot more popular than forgiveness. When we are mistreated by others, we respond with anger, hatred, and verbal or physical violence. We have a choice. We can react as a human self—with revenge; or respond as a spiritual self—with compassion and love.

To do what Jesus asks, when persecuted we are to confront anger and hate, and, rather than defending and protecting ourselves, we are to move toward true forgiveness and love of that person. That is the radical compassion preached by Jesus.

Jesus goes on to tell us that with compassion we not only pray for ourselves and our families, but even for our persecutors. He prompts us to go the extra mile and give others our coat when they ask only for a shirt.

Themes for Teens   The following themes from the Scriptures relate to the lives of teens:
- Be compassionate—forgive.
- Give up "an-eye-for-an-eye" living.
- Love your enemies.
- Turn the other cheek.
- Go the extra mile.

Our Response

Activity   **Journaling with the Scriptures**

These journal reflections are keyed to all the readings. They are designed to help the young people explore the readings more deeply day by day for an entire week.

Give each teen a copy of this week's readings and a copy of the following journal questions. Urge them to set aside some quiet time each day this week to reread the readings, reflect on the question for the day, and write in their journal.

Sunday. What does it mean when we say, "It is easier to make a fist than to reach out with an open hand"?

Monday. What does your spiritual self look like? What would you like it to look like?

Tuesday. Give examples of how you can "'do good to those who hate you; bless those who curse you and pray for those who maltreat you.'"

Wednesday. What happens when people hold a grudge? How does it destroy a relationship? Are you holding a grudge against anyone right now? What do you need to do to let go of it?

Thursday. Do you have any enemies? If not, are there people you don't like very much because they have treated you unfairly? Is there a family member you don't get along with too well? Is there a teacher at school who just drives you crazy? Pick one of these people and write a prayer for her or him.

Friday. All these readings show us the compassion and forgiveness of God. Take a few moments to bring your failings to God. What would you like to ask forgiveness for?

Saturday. Write the refrain of today's psalm in your journal. Rewrite the verses in your own words, thanking God for compassion and forgiveness in your life.

Activity Ideas

The following activity ideas also relate to the Scripture readings. You may want to read the passage(s) indicated as part of the activity.

- Who are our enemies? When we pray prayers of petition at Mass, we often pray for family and friends, for those who are sick, and for those in need. Invite the young people to join you in shared prayer for those we rarely pray for—our enemies. (Luke 6:27–38; 1 Sam. 26:2,7–9,12–13,22–23)

- We can find examples of an eye-for-an-eye living all around us in our everyday world. Ask the teens to bring in tapes or CDs of songs with the theme, "I will love you only if . . . ." Start a discussion with the question: "Could you imagine Jesus singing this song? Why or why not?" (Luke 6:27–38)

- What would it be like if we responded to Jesus' challenge to turn the other cheek? How would it be a radical change from the way we normally deal with other people? Divide the teens into groups of three or four. Instruct them to choose a situation from school or home in which radical forgiveness is needed. Ask them to plan and present short role-plays on how different the situation would be if we could turn the other cheek. (Luke 6:27–38; Ps. 103:1–2,3–4,8,10,12–13)

- Read the last few verses of the Gospel passage. How is this message similar to the Prayer of Saint Francis? Pray or sing the Prayer of Saint Francis at the close of your session on this week's readings. (Luke 6:27–38)

Eighth Sunday of the Year

Scripture Readings (85)

- ❖ Sir. 27:4–7
- ❖ Ps. 92:2–3,13–14,15–16
- ❖ 1 Cor. 15:54–58
- ❖ Luke 6:39–45

God's Word

A major theme of the Scripture readings is "Serve God in word and deed."

You may have heard the saying, "Actions speak louder than words," but today's reading from Sirach reminds us that we need to pay attention to our words as well. Sirach uses three symbols—a sieve, a potter's kiln, and the fruit of a tree— to show us that what a person says tells you a lot about what is in her or his heart. We get to know people by talking with them and listening to what they have to say. What might hurtful, bad, or profane speech say about what is in our heart?

The psalm tells us that one way to make good use of our speech is to use it to give thanks to God—morning, noon, and night. Images of nature, particularly trees, feature prominently in all of today's readings. Those that "are planted in the house of the Lord" flourish and bear fruit.

The second reading reminds us that Jesus is the fulfillment of the Scriptures. The Resurrection of Jesus is our victory over sin and death. Being a Christian is tough, but it is worth it. We need to persevere when times get tough. Christ has already won the victory, so we have no reason to despair.

The Gospel uses three analogies to warn us against being hypocrites. First, the example of the blind guide shows us that we must first learn to see ourselves before we can guide others. Second, the plank and speck example warns us that it is easier to find fault in others than to recognize our own failings. Third, a decayed tree and decayed fruit are used to describe the outcome of a person's life when evil rather than goodness prevails.

All three examples remind us to look at the fruit of our actions. Here we see that integrity between actions and words is important in the way we live our life, especially in our relationships with others.

Themes for Teens   The following themes from the Scriptures relate to the lives of teens:
- Actions speak as loud as words.
- Watch what you say and do.
- Bear fruit for the Lord.
- Take the plank out of your eye.
- Don't be a hypocrite.

Our Response

Activity   **Jesus in Word and Deed**

These games and the Scripture study offer a fun way for the teens to identify Jesus' message in all of today's readings by exploring his words and actions and what we can learn from them.

Introduce the activity with the following or similar words:

> Today's readings show us that we can learn a lot about a person by looking at his or her words and actions. What we say and what we do are important. What can we learn about Jesus by looking at what he said and did as we read the Gospels? Because our church year is exploring the Gospel of Luke in some detail, let's stick with Luke.

Divide the teens into small groups and give each group a Bible. Ask each group to search for three examples of things Jesus did and said.

Next, ask each group to pick one of Jesus' actions and prepare to act it out as in charades. For Jesus' words, the groups should prepare three crossword-puzzle-type clues.

When a group takes a turn, it should first act out the charade without words until the others guess what Jesus did. For what Jesus said, they should ask the rest of the group members to fill in the crossword letter boxes by using the clues given to them until they guess the phrase.

After a group guesses each answer, ask: "What does this word or action tell us about Jesus? What does it tell us about how we need to speak or act?"

Activity Ideas   The following activity ideas also relate to the Scripture readings. You may want to read the passage(s) indicated as part of the activity.

- Ask the young people to write answers to the following questions in their journal: "How does the saying, 'think before you speak' relate to today's first reading? When did you wish you had thought before you harmed another with your words? Describe this time." (Sir. 27:4–7)

- Challenge the teens to take a look at how they bear fruit on their family tree. Bring a small, indoor potted tree to your meeting and place it in the middle of your circle. Give each teen a piece of construction paper cut in the shape of a fruit, with yarn looped through the top. After reading today's Gospel together, ask the teens to write on the piece of paper fruit one way they bear fruit in their family. After the teens share their answers, ask them to add their pieces of fruit to the tree. (Luke 6:39–45)

- Use the following as a basis for a quiet-time reflection: "Jesus was crucified on a cross made from wood, made from a tree. How does this tree figure into the promise of our salvation?" (All readings)

- Today's psalm calls on us to thank God for many blessings. Hang a large piece of butcher paper on the wall of your meeting space. Instruct the teens to decorate it like a large Thanksgiving Day table, leaving room on the tablecloth for writing. Ask each teen to think of one blessing, offer thanks to God, and write it on the poster. (Ps. 92:2–3,13–14,15–16)

Ninth Sunday of the Year

Scripture Readings (88)

- ❖ 1 Kings 8:41–43
- ❖ Ps. 117:1,2
- ❖ Gal. 1:1–2,6–10
- ❖ Luke 7:1–10

God's Word

A major theme of the Scripture readings is "Welcome the stranger."

In the first reading, Solomon calls on God to grant blessings to foreigners and strangers, not just to the Chosen People of Israel. His prayer dedicates the Temple as a place open to all. To be witnesses to the world, to unite all under one God, we are to welcome all into God's house.

Psalm 117 is the shortest psalm in the Book of Psalms. It continues the theme of the first reading—that God's word is for the entire world. We must share the Good News with everyone. The Good News is not to be kept secret or locked behind church doors after Mass is over. It is to be shared by all who wish to hear it and live it.

Paul, writing in frustration to the Galatians, is speaking to Gentiles who have heard the Good News but are distracted by competing messages and are not sure who to believe anymore. Paul cannot be everywhere at once, and when he is gone, others try to undermine Jesus' message and put their own spin on the Gospel. In this letter Paul strongly upholds the message of Jesus. The last part of this letter reminds us that pleasing others, going along with the crowd, is the easy way out. Following Christ is the tougher choice, but the right choice.

In today's Gospel reading, a centurion begs a favor of Jesus—to save the life of a sick servant. The centurion is not a Jew. He is part of the occupying force, a foreigner not welcome in the land of Israel.

The centurion, knowing the attitude of the Jews toward foreigners, does not feel it proper even to approach Jesus, yet Jesus does not turn him away just because he is a foreigner. Impressed by the centurion's faith—which Jesus wishes could be found among the Israelites—Jesus makes the centurion's servant well.

Jesus welcomes outcasts, sinners, and foreigners throughout the Gospels. The elders ask Jesus to help the centurion because of his actions on behalf of the Jews. He has shown compassion and camaraderie with the people. Jesus is more impressed by the soldier's faith and behavior than by his religious and civil status.

At Mass, before receiving the Eucharist, we pray like the centurion: "Lord, I am not worthy to receive you, but only say the word and I shall be healed."

Themes for Teens   The following themes from the Scriptures relate to the lives of teens:
- The Good News is for all to hear.
- Welcome the stranger.
- Share the Good News.
- Jesus has power over death.
- You are welcome here.

Our Response

Activity   **Tell Me God's Story**

This activity is keyed to the readings as a whole. Through outreach and evangelization, it challenges the young people to find creative ways to share the Good News with younger children in their family or parish.

Give small groups of teens a two-week period to share the Good News with a child or a group of children. You may want to invite some primary-school religious educators to give the teens some ideas for using such things as songs, crafts, storytelling, or puppetry. The teens can do this project with younger siblings or with children in the community.

After two weeks, invite the teens to share with the entire group their experiences of sharing God's word. Ask questions like these:
- How did you try to share the Good News?
- What creative approaches did you use?
- How did the children react?
- What did you learn from this experience?

Activity Ideas   The following activity ideas also relate to the Scripture readings. You may want to read the passage(s) indicated as part of the activity.

- Some people think modern technology distracts us from faith in God. Challenge the teens to think of ways new communication technology—such as Web pages, cellular phones, and CD players—can be used as tools of evangelization. How can technology help us do what the psalm says, "Go out to all the world, and tell the Good News"? (Ps. 117:1,2)

- Why are we afraid of people who are strange or different? Are they only strange because we haven't yet had a chance to get to know them? If your group of teens is fairly new to one another, ask them to switch seats and spend the meeting working with and getting to know a new person. (Luke 7:1–10)

- Start a youth group buddy system for new teens who arrive in your parish. A teen "buddy" invites a new teen to the first youth group meeting, offers to sit with him or her at Mass, and calls him or her about each upcoming event. One key job of the buddy is to introduce the newcomer to other young people in the parish. (Luke 7:1–10)

- Ask permission to put messages in the windows of your church school, so that they can be seen by those passing by outside. The messages, completed by the teens, should say, "The Good News about Jesus is . . ." If a limited number of windows is available, the message could be changed every week for a few months. (Ps. 117:1,2)

Tenth Sunday of the Year

**Scripture Readings
(91)**

❖ 1 Kings 17:17–24
❖ Ps. 30:2,4,5–6,11,12,13
❖ Gal. 1:11–19
❖ Luke 7:11–17

God's Word

A major theme of the Scripture readings is "Lifesavers in the Scriptures."

In both the first reading and the Gospel today, we see God's mercy toward mothers who have lost children to death.

In the first reading, the mother asks the prophet Elijah to intercede for her. Elijah calls out to God to bring life back to the boy, and the child returns to life. This miracle is a sign of God's compassion. It is also an affirmation that God works through Elijah, and that the prophet is empowered to speak the word of God. The widow says, "'the word of the Lord comes truly from your mouth.'" Just as God did through Elijah, God also speaks and acts through each of us.

We cannot tell from reading this psalm what misfortune befell the psalmist, but God is given the title of rescuer. The widow from the first reading could have prayed this psalm, for surely when her son was restored, she was able to feel that the Lord had "changed [her] mourning into dancing."

In the second reading, Paul gives witness to the life he had before conversion and to how radically the Gospel has changed him. Well trained in Jewish tradition, Paul is so zealous in his faith that he persecutes members of the early church. Yet when God reveals Jesus to Paul, Paul's entire life is changed, and he travels everywhere to tell everyone about Jesus.

In the third reading, a miracle story from Luke's Gospel, Jesus reveals the power of God working through him when he takes pity on the widow and brings her son back to life. This is one of three miracles in the Gospels where Jesus restores life to someone who is dead.

The young man, perhaps a teenager, is the only son of the widow. Jesus, with the power of God, removes the source of her grief.

In both readings, the word of life is spoken from God through Elijah and then through Jesus. While earthly life is restored, we also have the promise of eternity.

Themes for Teens

The following themes from the Scriptures relate to the lives of teens:
• Jesus is our lifesaver.
• God comes to our rescue.
• Jesus has power over death.
• The word of God saves.
• Jesus can turn your life around.

Our Response

Activity

Live, from the Gospel!

This activity invites the young people to step inside the story of the Gospels and relive part of the experience of the people who walked and talked with Jesus.

Divide the teens into groups of five and ask the groups to assign a different one of the following roles to each person in their group: Jesus, the widow, the widow's son who was raised, a TV reporter, and a TV cameraperson.

Direct each group to put together a skit placing the Gospel story in modern times, and then interview the key players. The camera crew is the first to arrive on the scene after the miracle and is about to interview the son who has been raised and get his mother's reaction.

After all the teens are ready, invite each group to share with the others its version of the miraculous events.

Activity Ideas

The following activity ideas also relate to the Scripture readings. You may want to read the passage(s) indicated as part of the activity.

- After sharing today's Gospel, give each teen a roll of Life Savers candy with these questions attached: "How has God rescued you? How is faith in God a little like a life preserver?" Give the teens some quiet time for this sweet reflection. (Luke 7:11–17)

- Ask the teens to place themselves in today's Gospel and to write a response to the following question in their journal: "How would you feel if Jesus came up to you—as he did to the widow in today's Gospel—and said, 'Do not cry'"? (Luke 7:11–17)

- What can today's readings teach us about respect for life? If your school has a Respect Life group or your parish has someone in charge of Respect Life efforts, ask that person to come to your gathering to talk about ways teens can show respect for all life. (All readings)

- Jesus restores life to a widow's son, one of many miracles in the Gospels. Invite the teens in small groups to scour the Gospels looking for other miracles of Jesus. (Luke 7:11–17)

Eleventh Sunday of the Year

Scripture Readings (94)

- ❖ 2 Sam. 12:7–10,13
- ❖ Ps. 32:1–2,5,7,11
- ❖ Gal. 2:16,19–21
- ❖ Luke 7:36—8:3

God's Word

A major theme of the Scripture readings is "Celebrating God's forgiveness."

In the first reading, Nathan the prophet confronts David about his sins. These are not petty crimes: they include murder and adultery. Faced with Nathan's accusation, David admits, or confesses, his sin. Nathan, speaking on God's behalf, tells David, "'The Lord . . . has forgiven your sin.'" This reading from the Hebrew Scriptures shows that the sacrament of reconciliation has deep roots. When we celebrate the sacrament, we confess our sins and God forgives us through an intermediary—the priest.

The psalm sounds like the kind of prayer David might have said after his conversation with Nathan. The second verse includes a confession and a statement about the Lord's forgiveness. The first step to being forgiven is to admit our failings and to be willing to pray with an open heart: "Lord, forgive the wrong I have done."

The second reading today is one of many examples chronicled in early church writings of the tug-of-war that went on about the place of Jewish Law in Christianity. Paul makes it quite clear that only God puts us in right relationship with God and that this justification is available to all who have faith (trust) in Jesus Christ. This reading includes the powerful statement of faith: Once we truly believe in Christ, our life is not our own; it belongs to Jesus.

In the reading from Luke's Gospel, we see a contrast between the rude and inhospitable behavior of a Pharisee and the outpouring of love from a woman seeking forgiveness. In this Gospel the woman does not confess her sins verbally. She shows her deep love for Jesus by wiping his feet with her hair, washing them with her tears, and anointing them with oil. The Pharisee could not believe that Jesus would let a sinner touch him. Besides forgiving the woman, Jesus shares the story of the moneylender to try to teach the Pharisee—and us—about the true value of forgiveness.

All of today's readings celebrate forgiveness. Salvation does not come from following the law but from God's loving forgiveness. We need to recognize our failures and seek reconciliation. Our forgiveness comes from a personal relationship with a loving God.

Themes for Teens

The following themes from the Scriptures relate to the lives of teens:
- The Lord forgives you.
- Lord, forgive me.
- Sin is not in.
- Your faith will save you.
- God loves our sins away.

Our Response

Activity   What Is Wrong with This Picture?

This game and discussion activity is keyed to the readings as a whole. It helps us to see that Jesus looks at the world in a different way, and that we need to look at others through the eyes of forgiveness.

Give the young people copies of the picture found on page 30 and ask them to find ten things that are missing or wrong with the picture.

After the teens find all the mistakes, ask them to look at today's Gospel passage through the eyes of the Pharisee. From the Pharisee's point of view, what was wrong with this picture painted by Jesus?

Have the young people discuss the following questions:
- Why do we need to learn to look at the world through the eyes of Jesus?
- How would things look differently?
- How would our world change if we looked at it through the eyes of love? through the eyes of forgiveness?

Activity Ideas

The following activity ideas also relate to the Scripture readings. You may want to read the passage(s) indicated as part of the activity.

- Teens, like many adults, may be afraid of receiving the sacrament of reconciliation. Some may even be afraid of asking questions about this sometimes mysterious sacrament. Ask the teens to write questions—without using their names—that address their fears and uncertainties about the sacrament. Invite a parish or school priest to talk to them in an informal session to answer some of their questions. (Luke 7:36—8:3)

- Explain to the teens the value of an examination of conscience. You may want to share some you have found valuable over the years. In pairs, ask the teens to brainstorm some questions based on their experience at home, school, work, and in the parish. Gather all the questions together and distribute them in a small booklet for the teens to keep and use the next time they are preparing to receive the sacrament of reconciliation. (All readings)

- How do we build our conscience? Give each teen a large building block made of wood. Ask them to cover the block with white paper and then to write on it some ways they think we can build our conscience. As a large group, invite them to share one example from their block. As they finish, use the blocks to spell out the word *conscience* in block letters on the floor of your meeting space. (All readings)

- Ask the teens to answer the following question in their journal: "If one of your friends confronted you with what you had done wrong—like Nathan did to David—how would you react?" (2 Sam. 12:7–10,13)

Twelfth Sunday of the Year

Scripture Readings (97)

- ❖ Zech. 12:10–11
- ❖ Ps. 63:2,3–4,5–6,8–9
- ❖ Gal. 3:26–29
- ❖ Luke 9:18–24

God's Word

A major theme of the Scripture readings is "Suffering Messiah."

In Zechariah, grace is poured out on the people, and they mourn the one they have put to death. Christians sometimes point to this text, saying that it foreshadows the kind of death the Messiah experienced—crucifixion.

The responsorial psalm describes a need for God so great that it is compared to a thirst that is difficult to quench. Have you ever been very thirsty, your mouth so dry that you couldn't wait for a cool drink of water? The psalmist cries out from the desert of his soul, thirsting for God to fill the emptiness. The rest of the psalm is a prayer of blessing and thanksgiving. It also teaches us how to approach our God, lifting up our hands and voice in prayer.

The second reading tells us that our faith unites us rather than divides us. Our divisions are our own creation. God does not discriminate. Christ brings us all together in one family through our baptism into his death.

As we join the Gospel of Luke at this point, rumors are flying about the identity of Jesus. The crowds are not really sure—prophet? follower of John the Baptist? When Peter comes up with the right answer, Jesus commands that it be kept a secret. Then, as in the first reading, Jesus reveals the type of death he will suffer. Jesus is not the type of messiah they expected. Still worse, Jesus tells the followers they must carry the same cross and suffer for his sake.

The people had dreamed of a messiah to save them from their troubles. The last thing they wished for was a suffering messiah. God reveals the plan for Jesus and for each of us. Discipleship is more than martyrdom; it also includes daily suffering, often referred to as "carrying our own cross."

Themes for Teens The following themes from the Scriptures relate to the lives of teens:
- Carry the cross with Jesus
- Put on Christ.
- Who do you say Jesus is?
- Quench your thirst with God.
- God doesn't discriminate.

Our Response

Activity **The Cross Will Find Us**

This mini-retreat is keyed to the first reading and the Gospel. It offers several activities that invite the young people to better understand what it means to "carry our cross" in everyday life. The activities can be arranged to fit either a half-day or a full-day retreat.

Here are some possible sessions to include in your retreat:
- *Discussion.* Discuss these questions: "If you had a choice between following someone who would give you money and all the things you wanted and following someone who would cause you to suffer, who would you pick? Why didn't the Apostles flee? Why did they decide to go along with Jesus and help carry his cross?"
- *Journal reflection.* "In our lives we don't have to seek the cross, it will find us." Ask the teens: "What does this mean? How does it apply to your life?"
- *Retreat keepsake.* Give each teen a "cross in my pocket" devotion that they can carry with them to remember today's readings.
- *Poster project.* Give the teens each a piece of 8½-by-11-inch sheet of paper. Ask them to write examples of some of the burdens and sufferings in their own life and in the lives of their family and friends. Have the teens share their examples in small groups; then tape them to the wall in the shape of a cross.
- *Witness talk.* Ask one teen and one adult to give short witness talks on the following theme: "What does it mean to take up your cross each day?"
- *Prayer service.* Locate a large cross that is quite heavy but can be held by one person for a short time. For shared prayer, ask the teens to take turns holding the cross and offering a prayer of petition for help with the crosses they have to carry in their life.
- *Pilgrimage.* Ask the teens to get together to carry—for some distance—the same cross they held alone. Then ask: "How does helping one another make it easier to carry our crosses? How can we help one another carry our crosses?"

Activity Ideas The following activity ideas also relate to the Scripture readings. You may want to read the passage(s) indicated as part of the activity.

- Is it true that you can tell a lot about someone from what they wear? Ask the teens to list some of the messages found on the T-shirts they own. What do the messages tell us about them? Ask: "If you were 'clothed in Christ,' what would your T-shirt say?" Buy some plain white T-shirts and fabric paint, and ask the teens to design their own "witness wear." (Gal. 3:26–29)

- Choose several activities from the retreat "Who Do You Say That I Am?" in *Vine and Branches 2,* by Maryann Hakowski (Winona, MN: Saint Mary's Press, 1992) to help the teens answer, with Peter, the question raised by Jesus in today's Gospel. (Luke 9:18–24)

- As an icebreaker before discussion of today's readings, ask the teens to write a slogan, parodying contemporary drink commercials, on how we can quench our thirst with God. For example, instead of "Things go better with Coke," the slogan could say, "Things go better with God." (Zech. 12:10–11; Ps. 63:2,3–4,5–6,8–9)

- Ask the teens to learn more about their baptism day from their parents. Invite them to bring in photos and their baptismal outfit if possible. After a chance for storytelling and show-and-tell, ask the following questions: "What does the white garment of baptism symbolize? How do we 'put on Christ' when we are baptized?" (Gal. 3:26–29)

- Discuss with the teens the mystery of suffering: "Why did Christ suffer? Why did Christ associate suffering with being his follower?"

Thirteenth Sunday of the Year

Scripture Readings (100)
- ❖ 1 Kings 19:16,19–21
- ❖ Ps. 16:1–2,5,7–8,9–10,11
- ❖ Gal. 5:1,13–18
- ❖ Luke 9:51–62

God's Word

A major theme of the Scripture readings is "Radical commitment."

In First Kings, Elisha gives up a herd of oxen and leaves his family behind in order to follow Elijah and learn how to be a prophet. His enthusiasm and unwavering allegiance are powerful examples of saying yes to God.

The psalmist professes trust and confidence in God. We need not want for material goods when we have the Lord as our inheritance.

In Paul's Letter to the Galatians, we learn that being a Christian means living by the Spirit and giving up the desires of the flesh. Paul saw a community filled with infighting. This reading explains that freedom does not mean that we can do whatever we want. If we love Jesus, we need to care for others. The commandment "Love your neighbor as yourself" is the answer.

This week's reading from the Gospel of Luke is the beginning of Jesus' journey to Jerusalem. It stresses the urgency of the journey and Jesus' commitment to it. The response of Jesus to those who would follow him seems pretty harsh. How could Jesus, known for compassion, not allow a potential follower to bury his father or to say good-bye to loved ones? But for followers of Jesus, the commitment to the journey to Jerusalem—the journey of life—is equally urgent.

Following Jesus is a radical commitment. To do so with fidelity to our call we have to give up our past for an uncertain future, trusting that Jesus will guide us on our journey to Jerusalem, the journey to God.

Themes for Teens

The following themes from the Scriptures relate to the lives of teens:
- Journey to Jerusalem.
- Journey with Jesus.
- Christianity is a radical commitment.
- Be a radical Christian.
- Freedom comes with responsibility.

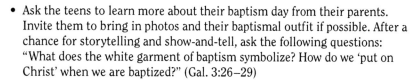

Ordinary Time

Our Response

Activity

Pilgrimage Hike

This walk and reflection activity introduces the young people to the devotion called a pilgrimage and offers them an active way to reflect on all the readings.

Send the teens a ticket, possibly made to look like a train or airline ticket, with an invitation that says, "You are invited to walk with us to Jerusalem."

Before leaving, discuss with the teens what a pilgrimage is and how it is a popular spiritual devotion in many countries.

Take a hike, with the goal being to learn more about Jesus along the way. Plan at least four stops. At each stop read one of today's readings and reflect as a group on the following questions: "How can we walk with Jesus to Jerusalem? How can we be more open to learning Jesus' words and ways?" You may also want to plan for singing along the route.

Activity Ideas

The following activity ideas also relate to the Scripture readings. You may want to read the passage(s) indicated as part of the activity.

- Pack and unpack for your journey to Jerusalem. Place an old, empty suitcase in the middle of your discussion space. Ask the teens to think of what they would need to take with them on their journey: "What do we need to pack and unpack if we make a decision to follow Jesus?" (1 Kings 19:16, 19–21; Ps. 16:1–2,5,7–8,9–10,11; Luke 9:51–62)

- Play a version of musical chairs called Excuses, Excuses, with two or three chairs missing. Those left standing have to name one excuse given for not following Jesus. Talk later about how we need to stop making excuses for neglecting our relationship with God. (Luke 9:51–62)

- After reading today's Scripture readings, teach the teens a song with a journey message. Some possibilities include: "Companions on a Journey" (*Companions on a Journey* [Chicago: GIA Pubilications, 1985]) or "Come and Journey" (*Come and Journey* [Phoenix, AZ: North American Liturgy Resources, 1985]), both by David Haas. Ask the teens for their own examples of journey songs. (Luke 9:51–62)

- Give each teen play money with the following question written on the back of it: "What is the cost of discipleship?" Have them share their answers in pairs. (All readings)

Fourteenth Sunday of the Year

Scripture Readings
(103)

- ❖ Isa. 66:10–14
- ❖ Ps. 66:1–3,4–5,6–7,16,20
- ❖ Gal. 6:14–18
- ❖ Luke 10:1–12,17–20

God's Word

A major theme of the Scripture readings is "Workers for the harvest."

The first reading is a great piece of poetry from Isaiah. In it Jerusalem is compared to a mother nursing and caring for her child. Besides a full stomach and the warmth of encircling arms, we are promised prosperity and wealth comparable to a never-ending river. A mother's love and a flowing river are two metaphors for God's never-ending love. God as mother is a strong image here, and it invites us to look at images of both mothers and fathers as a way to relate to our God.

Psalm 66 calls on the entire earth to "cry out to God with joy." How does the earth reflect the glory of God? Look around you—even the smallest bit of creation, by the magnificence of its unique design, celebrates God.

We brag about a lot of things—making the football team, buying nice clothes, getting good grades—but to brag about Jesus, to brag about the cross, must have seemed strange even to the early Christians. But Paul, the author of this letter to the Galatians, is so excited to be a Christian that nothing else matters. He says that only those who suffer with Jesus can boast of anything, because it is the cross of Christ that brings about a new creation.

In today's Gospel reading, Jesus adds seventy-two disciples to the original twelve, gives them instructions, and sends them out to do God's work. Jesus compares himself to a farmer with a large harvest ahead and not enough workers to bring the crops in. He needs help with the harvest of the Reign of God.

The seventy-two come back really psyched. Even demons were no match for the name of Jesus. Jesus talks to them about the wolves among lambs to remind them that they will not always be so well received. Jesus does not want their newfound power to go to their head, and he cautions them to remember what their real mission is and to set their eyes on heaven.

Themes for Teens

The following themes from the Scriptures relate to the lives of teens:
- God comforts us.
- God loves us like a mother.
- Brag about God!
- Help with the harvest.
- Disciples don't need gear, only courage.

Our Response

Activity

The Hands and Feet of God

This craft and prayer activity is keyed to the Gospel reading. It includes the teens in the mission of the seventy-two and urges them to reach out in ministry through prayer and action.

Introduce the activity by saying the following:

> Jesus sends the seventy-two out to places where he would be going. What are some of the places in our community and the world where we should be going for Jesus? Jesus' disciples were called to reach, heal, and teach. How can we do each of these things?

Ask the teens to trace their footprints, cut them out, and write on them one way that we can be the feet of God. Give examples. Put them up on a large bulletin board with the saying, "We are the feet of God."

Next, ask the young people to trace and cut out their handprints and write their own name on them. Mix them up and distribute them, making sure no teen receives her or his own handprints. Then say:

> Jesus told the disciples to travel in pairs. This week pray for one of your fellow Christians. Make time each day to pray for him or her. You can do so by reflecting on and praying this week's Gospel for the person.

Urge the teens to place a hand bookmark in their Bible or bookbag as a reminder of who their prayer partner is for the week.

Activity Ideas The following activity ideas also relate to the Scripture readings. You may want to read the passage(s) indicated as part of the activity.

- God is often referred to as "Father." Ask the teens how they feel when God is talked about as "Mother."

  After sharing today's first reading, invite the teens to pray the Lord's Prayer, but begin it with "Our Mother, who is in heaven . . ." Ask for their reaction: "What is strange about praying this way? What is comforting about it?" (Isa. 66:10–14)

- How do we "cry out to God with joy"? Divide the teens into cheerleading squads of five to six people, and ask each group to come up with a cheer for God to share with the others. (Ps. 66:1–3,4–5,6–7,16,20)

- Read the beautiful blessing at the end of Galatians: "May the favor of our Lord Jesus Christ be with your spirit." Ask the teens to reflect in their journal on the following questions:
  - ○ What does this blessing mean?
  - ○ How would you say it in your own words?
  - ○ Who would you like to pray this blessing for right now?

  (Gal. 6:14–18)

- Put together a group brag book about God. Give each teen a page to write on and decorate. Use a three-hole punch to collect all of them in a binder to share and revisit. (Gal. 6:14–18)

Fifteenth Sunday of the Year

Scripture Readings (106)
- ❖ Deut. 30:10–14
- ❖ Ps. 69:14,17,30–31,33–34,36,37
- ❖ Col. 1:15–20
- ❖ Luke 10:25–37

God's Word

A major theme of the Scripture readings is "Who is my neighbor?"

All of today's readings deal with how to follow God and how to live the life God wants us to live.

In the Book of Deuteronomy, Moses tells us to listen to the voice of God and to follow God with our heart and soul. Sometimes we may feel like God is distant and far away. Moses tells us that God's commandment is not up in the sky or across the sea. We don't need to take the space shuttle to find God's will. We don't need to book passage on an oceanliner to follow God's command. Moses tells us that the word of God is already in our mouth and in our heart. It is up to us to speak and live God's word.

The psalmist says that we should turn to God whenever we are in need. The psalm reminds us that prayer is a key part of our relationship with God.

Found in this one psalm are several forms of prayer—prayers for mercy, favor, protection, and help in affliction; prayers of praise and thanksgiving; and prayers for the poor and for those in prison.

The second reading contains an early Christian hymn in praise of Jesus. In it Jesus is compared to Wisdom, who was present with God at creation. Jesus is presented here as the image of God, as being as powerful as God, and also as Creator. The church is called the Body, with Christ as the head. Finally, Jesus is the source of all reconciliation, and the cross is the source of all peace.

In the reading from Luke's Gospel, a lawyer wants the formula for ever-lasting life. Jesus answers a question with a question. The lawyer replies that we must love God with our heart, soul, strength, and mind, and we must also love our neighbor as ourselves. This lawyer surely knows the Law and the Commandments, but he is a bit fuzzy on who exactly is our neighbor.

Jesus answers the question of "Who is my neighbor?" with the parable of the good Samaritan: A traveler is robbed while on a journey. Two people come by—a priest and a Levite—yet they walk right by without helping because they believe that touching a Samaritan will make them impure and prevent them from participating in Jewish ritual. A Samaritan (a religious and social outcast in the eyes of the Jews) not only stops to help but stays with the man and makes sure he is all right.

Too many people today are like the first two. They walk by, believing that ritual is more important than caring for people. Jesus asks us to be the person who stops, who makes time to care for someone in need, a care that is a pre-requisite for authentic ritual. The answer to the question "Who is my neighbor?" is "Anyone who is in need."

Themes for Teens

The following themes from the Scriptures relate to the lives of teens:
- God is in your heart.
- Ask God for help.
- God is there when you need help.
- Jesus is God.
- Be a good Samaritan.

Our Response

Activity   Who Is My Neighbor?

This prayer service is keyed to the Gospel reading. It connects the parable of the good Samaritan with events in our own community and world.
- *Preparation.* Collect articles recently published in your local newspaper. You will need one about a robbery, one about a beating, two examples of times when people failed to help, and three examples of times when people did help. Ask two teens to prepare to read the parts of Reader 1 and Reader 2.
- *Call to prayer.* Invite the teens to participate in the following prayer:

Reader 1.   There was a man going down from Jerusalem to Jericho who fell in with robbers.
Reader 2.   [Read the newspaper clipping about someone who was robbed.]
Response.   So what? These things happen all the time.

Reader 1.   They stripped him, beat him, and then went off leaving him half dead.
Reader 2.   [Read the newspaper clipping about someone who has been assaulted.]
Response.   Why should I care? He isn't my neighbor.

Ordinary Time

Reader 1. A priest happened to be going down the same road; he saw the injured man but continued on.

Reader 2. [Read the first newspaper clipping about someone who failed to help.]

Response. Why should I stop? This person isn't a member of my family.

Reader 1. Likewise, there was a Levite who came the same way; he saw him but went on.

Reader 2. [Read the second newspaper clipping about someone who failed to help.]

Response. I don't have time. Someone else will stop.

Reader 1. But a Samaritan who was journeying along came on him and was moved to pity at the sight. He approached him and dressed his wounds, pouring oil and wine as a means to heal.

Reader 2. [Read the first newspaper clipping about someone who makes a difference by helping others.]

Response. Lord, help me to see all who are my neighbors.

Reader 1. He then hoisted him onto his own beast and brought him to an inn where he cared for him.

Reader 2. [Read the second newspaper clipping about someone who makes a difference by helping others.]

Response. Lord, help me to see that all are my family.

Reader 1. The next day he took out two silver pieces and gave them to the innkeeper with the request, "Look after him, and if there is any further expense, I will repay you on my way back."

Reader 2. [Read the third newspaper clipping about someone who makes a difference by helping others.]

Response. Lord, help me to be a good Samaritan.

- *Additional activity.* Ask the teens each to bring a newspaper to your meeting, and allow them to search for and clip out the articles needed for this prayer service.

Activity Ideas

The following activity ideas also relate to the Scripture readings. You may want to read the passage(s) indicated as part of the activity.

- Create a good Samaritan award at your parish or school to honor teens who serve others. So often teens get a bad rap. Here is a way to affirm them as well as to make the wider community aware of the good they can do. (Luke 10:25–37)

- Invite the teens to share stories about good Samaritans in their life, people who came to their aid when they most needed help. (Luke 10:25–37)

- Play one of these two icebreakers to get the young people thinking about the question, "Who is my neighbor?"
  ○ Play a game of dodge ball. The person throwing the ball yells, "Who is my neighbor?" As others dodge the ball, they yell, "Not me. Not me."
  ○ Play Samaritan ball toss. Before throwing the ball, call out, "Who is my neighbor?" The person catching the ball must identify a need in the community before throwing the ball to someone else.

(Luke 10:25–37)

- After reading the psalm, ask the teens to identify all the different types of prayers mentioned. Divide the teens into groups to write their own prayers based on the psalm themes. (Ps. 69:14,17,30–31,33–34,36,37)

Sixteenth Sunday of the Year

Scripture Readings (109)
- ❖ Gen. 18:1–10
- ❖ Ps. 15:2–3,3–4,5
- ❖ Col. 1:24–28
- ❖ Luke 10:38–42

God's Word

A major theme of the Scripture readings is "Welcome God in your life."

Abraham could work at a four-star hotel. He goes out of his way to make three traveling strangers feel welcome. Abraham runs to greet them and bows to show respect. He shows them to a shady spot and brings them water to bathe their feet. Only the best for the guests—a choice steer and fresh-baked rolls.

In the first reading, God appears to Abraham and Sarah through the three strangers. Their hospitality is rewarded when God blesses them with a long-wished-for child.

Just as Abraham and Sarah find God through their kindness to strangers, the psalmist says that acting with justice toward others will help us feel God's presence through those we help. The psalm includes a tough prescription for living. Being a just person includes being honest and avoiding gossip, refusing to harm anyone through word or action, and avoiding using money as a weapon.

In the Letter to the Colossians, Paul describes how suffering for Christ helps to reveal who Jesus is. This reading celebrates Paul's call to serve God and others through ministry. Paul finds joy in serving God and others, even if it requires suffering. Just as we share in Jesus' Resurrection, we must also endure suffering in our life.

The Gospel reading continues this theme of hospitality with a visit by Jesus to the home of Martha and Mary. This passage is more than just an argument between Mary and Martha. It highlights the importance of listening to Jesus.

Both women show their hospitality to Jesus in different ways. Martha rushes around busily. She probably is preparing food, setting the table, and making sure everything is perfect. Mary leaves all the work to Martha and sits at Jesus' feet, soaking in all Jesus has to say. Martha resents getting stuck with all the housework and wants Jesus to tell Mary to help her. How surprised she must be when Jesus says that Mary, rather than Martha, has chosen the right thing to do!

Being present, spending time with a person, is how we truly make them feel welcome and at home.

Sitting at Jesus' feet, Mary is a model of discipleship. She shed the business of everyday life to reflect on the word of God. This reading also highlights listening to and proclaiming the word as important ministries. We need to understand the word of God before we can go out and minister to people in other ways.

Themes for Teens

The following themes from the Scriptures relate to the lives of teens:
- Welcome the stranger.
- We suffer with Jesus.
- Don't be too busy for God.
- Take time to listen to Jesus.
- Sit at the feet of Jesus.

Our Response

Activity   A Welcoming Community

This discussion activity is keyed to the readings as a whole. It asks the young people to take a close look at how they include others in their group and make them feel welcome.

Invite your group of teens to take this hospitality test. Determine if they pass or fail, and then ask, "What can we do to be more welcoming to others?"

Why Newcomers Return

1. Someone was there to greet me when I got out of the car and showed me exactly where to go.
2. When I walked in, there was an agenda on the door to let me know what was happening that night. I felt like I knew what was going on.
3. Right inside the door was a check-in table and somebody to show me around.
4. All the kids were wearing name tags—not just the new people. I didn't feel like "the new geek." People called me by name.
5. It was never boring! We were involved in the lesson; we didn't just watch some adult do and talk for us.
6. Everything seemed organized and ready before I got there. The adults were free to spend time with me.
7. There was plenty of game equipment for everyone. It wasn't beat up like it had come from somebody's junk closet.
8. People seem to really care about me. As I left, adults were at the door to say good-bye and ask me to come back next week.
9. Three days after I visited the group, I got a postcard in the mail inviting me back the next Sunday. The youth minister wrote it by hand!
10. Even though I wasn't a member of their church, I got a youth newsletter in the mail the very next month. It made me feel like I was included in their plans.

Why Newcomers Don't Come Back

1. I'd never been to that church before, and it took me 30 minutes to find the youth room!
2. My mom doesn't think I should go back because there were so many kids and only two or three adults. She didn't feel it was safe, and I really didn't either.
3. During the meeting, the leader made me go up front and tell the group lots of stuff about myself. I was TOTALLY embarrassed!
4. I didn't know what was going on, and I got in trouble for not being in the right place at the right time.
5. They must not have very much storage in that church because there sure was a lot of junk in the youth room.
6. Nobody sat with me. I felt all alone!
7. The leader called on me during lesson time. I'm not "Joe Christian," and I felt stupid.
8. The adults were clueless about what a teenager is up against today.
9. The group was in the middle of a long-term project; I wasn't able to join in on it.
10. They didn't talk much about God, and that's what I really needed.

(Caro, "Impressions," p. 45)

Activity Ideas

The following activity ideas also relate to the Scripture readings. You may want to read the passage(s) indicated as part of the activity.

- Encourage your group to create a Welcome Wagon for teens who are new to your parish or school. Some ideas include:
  - Introduce them to your pastor.
  - Sit with them at Mass.
  - Send them a calendar of upcoming events.
  - Remember them with a card on their birthday.
    (Gen. 18:1–10; Ps. 15:2–3,3–4,5; Luke 10:38–42)

- Join the adults in your parish to sponsor a welcome weekend for new parishioners. The teens can serve baked goods they made themselves and coffee and juice. They can do a craft project with or read stories to children while the parents register in the parish. (Gen. 18:1–10; Ps. 15:2–3,3–4,5; Luke 10:38–42)

- Play getting-to-know-you icebreakers, such as People Bingo, where you match people with fun facts about themselves and collect a different person's signature in each square; or Circle Introductions, where you greet each person—first nonverbally and then verbally—with a different greeting. (Gen. 18:1–10; Ps. 15:2–3,3–4,5; Luke 10:38–42)

- At the end of the week, direct the teens to reflect on the new people they met throughout the week. Ask them to write in their journal a little bit about each person they met and to answer the question, "How did I meet God through this person?" (Gen. 18:1–10)

Seventeenth Sunday of the Year

Scripture Readings (112)

- ❖ Gen. 18:20–32
- ❖ Ps. 138:1–2,2–3,6–7,7–8
- ❖ Col. 2:12–14
- ❖ Luke 11:1–13

God's Word

A major theme of the Scripture readings is "Persevere in prayer."

It is good for Abraham that God has a lot of patience. Abraham keeps asking God questions to test the limits of God's forgiveness and mercy. Life in Sodom and Gomorrah—two cities with reputations for evil—is getting out of hand. Abraham is pretty sure God is going to put an end to it, but he is also worried about the few in the city who might be innocent. But we learn that whether there are forty or thirty or ten innocent people, our just God will not punish them for the sins or crimes of all the others. Our God is a just, merciful, and compassionate God. We also learn from this reading that God is approachable. Abraham gives us a great model for prayer—that it should be a conversation between us and God.

The words of today's psalm are comforting. God hears us when we pray, and answers our prayers. The psalm reminds us that our conversations with

Ordinary Time

God cannot be just "gimme" prayers. Having seen God's response to prayer, the psalmist reacts with this prayer of praise and thanksgiving.

The writer of Colossians is trying to help followers understand baptism by connecting it with Jesus' death and Resurrection. Being "buried with [Christ]" in baptism might seem upsetting until we realize the promise of resurrection is ours as well. Going into the water symbolizes dying to an old way of life; coming out of the water symbolizes new life.

Like the last few Sundays, Jesus continues to teach followers how to be disciples. Today's lesson is on the power of prayer and how to pray. In the first part of today's Gospel reading, Jesus teaches the disciples how to pray, giving them the words to what we call the Lord's Prayer. This prayer is a treasury of different forms of prayer. When we pray "hallowed be your name," we offer a prayer of praise. "Give us each day our daily bread" is a prayer of petition. "Forgive us our sins" is a prayer of contrition. Throughout the prayer we profess and celebrate our faith.

Jesus then tells a story of a needy person who comes to the door in the middle of the night. Here we learn to be persistent in our prayer. Prayer is not a once-and-done event; it needs to be a regular part of our life.

Finally, God is portrayed as a loving father who cannot resist the prayers of needy children. We are to call God *Abba,* or "Daddy," stressing the close, intimate relationship God has with us. We are encouraged to approach God with whatever we need "'for whoever asks, receives; whoever seeks, finds; whoever knocks, is admitted.'"

Themes for Teens   The following themes from the Scriptures relate to the lives of teens:
- Prayer takes perseverance.
- Bring your needs to God.
- Make time to pray.
- God hears our prayers.

Our Response

Activity   **Ask, Seek, Knock**

This prayer service enables the young people to answer the invitation Jesus offers in today's Gospel: to approach God with all our needs.
- *Call to prayer.*
- *Opening song.* "Seek Ye First," by Karen Lafferty, verse 1, (*Today's Missal, Music Issue, 1997* [Portland, OR: Oregon Catholic Press], no. 494) or a similar song
- *First reading.* "'Ask and you shall receive; seek and you shall find; knock and it shall be opened to you.'"
- *Ask.* Give each teen a pipe cleaner. Ask the teens to think of a need or concern they would like to bring to God, to think of a symbol to represent the prayer, and then to shape the symbol with the pipe cleaner. When the teens are ready, invite them to come forward one at a time and place their symbol on the floor in the center of the prayer space.
- *Seek.* Tell the teens that Jesus assures us that if we search for what we need, we will find it. Ask them to share a verbal prayer of petition with the group. The response is, "God, we seek your help in our time of need."
- *Knock.* Jesus said: "'Knock, and [the door] shall be opened to you.'"

    Knocker. [Knock, knock, knock]
    Reader. Come in with your dreams.

    Knocker. [Knock, knock, knock]
    Reader. Enter, carrying your wishes and your longings.

Knocker. [Knock, knock, knock]
Reader. Open the door, you who are afraid or worried or weighed down.

Knocker. [Knock, knock, knock]
Reader. Bring your dreams, bring your hopes, bring your burdens.

Knocker. [Knock, knock, knock]
Reader. Bring them all here to be blessed and made holy.

Knocker. [Knock, knock, knock]
Reader. Bring them to me because they are you.

Knocker. [Knock, knock, knock]
Reader. Welcome. Be at home. Come in.

- *Second reading.* "'Ask and you shall receive; seek and you shall find; knock and it shall be opened to you.'"
- *Closing song.* "Seek Ye First," by Karen Lafferty, verse 2, or a similar song
(Hakowski, *Teaching Manual for PrayerWays,*
pp. 44–46 and handout 4–A)

Activity Ideas

The following activity ideas also relate to the Scripture readings. You may want to read the passage(s) indicated as part of the activity.

- Ask the teens to record their responses to this activity in their journal, with the following directions:
  - Draw a big question mark over a page of your journal. What question would you like to ask God about? Why? Write it and others inside the question mark. Draw a pair of binoculars or a telescope on another page in your journal. What are you seeking? Why? Finally, draw a door on another page of your journal. When you knock, what do you hope will be behind the door? Why?

(Luke 11:1–13)

- Invite the teens to share stories from their own life that reflect on how God answers prayers—but not always in the way we want or expect. Why is it important to keep praying even when we don't seem to get what we want right away? (Gen. 18:20–32; Luke 11:1–13)

- Talk about the difference between traditional recited prayer and spontaneous prayer. Why are both valuable? Give each small group of teens a different traditional prayer. Challenge them to rewrite the prayer in the form of a conversation with God. Share the dialog prayers with the entire group. (All readings)

- Teach the teens the Lord's Prayer in another language. Talk about how this universal prayer connects us with other Catholics and Christians throughout the world. (Luke 11:1–13)

Eighteenth Sunday of the Year

Scripture Readings (115)

- ❖ Eccles. 1:2; 2:21–23
- ❖ Ps. 95:1–2,6–7,8–9
- ❖ Col. 3:1–5,9–11
- ❖ Luke 12:13–21

God's Word

A major theme of the Scripture readings is "Wealth isn't everything."

Today's readings show us how all the wealth and possessions in the world actually have very little value when compared with growing rich in the sight of God.

In the first reading, a man spends all his time laboring under the sun. He has profit and prosperity, but he must also deal with anxiety, sorrow, and grief. This person seems a lot like today's workaholics—working long hours to buy a bigger house, a fancier car. We never seem to have enough. But what good is always wanting bigger and better of everything? "Vanity of vanities, says Qoheleth." We cannot find meaning in material things; we find meaning through a good relationship with our God.

The combination of the first reading and the psalm suggests that material things can "harden [our] heart." If our heart is hard—filled with everything except God—how can we possibly hear God's voice? The psalmist reminds us to make time for God, to sing joyfully, to thank God, to bow down in worship, and to be humble and kneel before God.

In the Letter to the Colossians, we see a strong contrast between living for the things of this earth and living for Christ. The writer asks us to "be intent on things above." Through baptism we give up our old selves and "put on Christ." Our old self has a lot to give up—evil desires, lying, lust. But the new self is one shaped in the image of God. No matter who we are or where we come from, Christ lives within us.

A man in this Gospel story tries to get Jesus to mediate a fight he is having with his brother over money and wealth. Instead, Jesus tells him he is wasting energy on the wrong things. Jesus tells the parable of the rich fool. This farmer has such a great harvest that he has to build bigger and bigger storage bins to hold it all. Sharing the extra with other people probably never crosses his mind.

But before the farmer has a chance to eat, drink, and be merry, God tells him his time is up. This guy finds out that the saying is true: "You can't take it with you." When God requires his life, he sure doesn't have much to show for it—just some bins full of grain and a lavish lifestyle.

All the readings today call us to have the right attitude about material possessions. Material possessions are not bad. It is how we use them or hoard them that can cause us trouble.

Themes for Teens

The following themes from the Scriptures relate to the lives of teens:
- You can't take it with you.
- Don't let possession possess you.
- Count your blessings, not your money.
- Bigger isn't always better.
- Set your heart on God.

Our Response

Activity   **Money, Money, Money**

This three-part discussion is keyed to the readings as a whole. It urges the young people to reflect on the attitudes toward materialism in today's society and on their own attitude about money and the collecting of material things.

Give the teens a slip of paper containing the following information and question: "An armored car is in an accident on the highway, and money starts flying around. You are standing nearby, and no one else is around. What would you do and why?" Ask the teens to pair up and share their answers.

Direct each pair of teens to join another pair for the second part of this discussion. Give each group three hundred dollars to spend on an imaginary trip to the mall. Give them 20 minutes for their shopping spree. You can provide catalogs as a help. Have them write down what they buy and how much it costs. After they share their shopping list with the whole group, ask them what they bought for other people, what they bought for the needy.

Invite one of the teens to read today's Gospel passage aloud. Allow a few minutes for reflection.

Ask each group of four teens to join another foursome to form groups of eight. Direct each group to rewrite the story, using modern language and experience. Close by asking the teens what they can do to change this story of materialism in our everyday lives.

Activity Ideas   The following activity ideas also relate to the Scripture readings. You may want to read the passage(s) indicated as part of the activity.

- Tape a TV episode of *Highway to Heaven* or *Touched by an Angel* and show it to your class. After viewing it, discuss in small groups: "How does God use other people to soften hard hearts?" (Ps. 95:1–2,6–7,8–9)

- Copy a page from a day planner or other schedule organizer book. Give the teens each a copy and ask them to map out an example of one of their busiest days of the week, including school, homework, sports, clubs, family chores, time with friends, and so on. Ask them to highlight the time set aside for God. Challenge them to make more time for God every day. (Ps. 95:1–2,6–7,8–9)

- Write a letter to God that inventories your blessings instead of your things. Thank God for all the wonderful blessings you have received. (All readings)

- Contrast *Lifestyles of the Rich and Famous* with a show your teens produce called *Lifestyles of the Poor and Humble* or *Lifestyles of the Poor in Spirit.* In small groups, the teens can act out examples from today's society where too much emphasis is placed on things at the expense of people. They can follow with another skit highlighting the kind of lifestyle Jesus calls us to in today's Gospel. (Luke 12:13–21)

Nineteenth Sunday of the Year

Scripture Readings (118)

- ❖ Wis. 18:6–9
- ❖ Ps. 33:1,12,18–19,20–22
- ❖ Heb. 11:1–2,8–19
- ❖ Luke 12:32–48

God's Word

A major theme of the Scripture readings is "Be ready; be faithful."

In the first reading from Wisdom, the people have faith that God will deliver them from their enemies. As they wait for God, they pray by offering sacrifices and living the way of God. The Israelites know God will fulfill all promises. God's faithfulness came through in the past, and it will help them build their future.

As in the first reading, the psalmist says that God has chosen us. But this relationship is not a one-way street. Even though God has chosen us, in order to have a relationship, we have to respond to God. We put our hope and confidence in God and pray for kindness and protection. This is the true meaning of faith.

The psalm says the eyes of God are upon us. How comforting to know that God is watching over us! Another image of God found in this psalm is one of a shield, protecting us from danger. The psalmist speaks of the yearning for God that we all experience at one time or another: "Our soul waits for the Lord."

The second reading recalls the example of faith set by Abraham and Sarah. Abraham followed where God led and obeyed all commands. Abraham was even willing to sacrifice his son, Isaac, if that was what God required. Another theme of this reading is trusting in what we may not be able to see. Abraham and Sarah's descendants did not all live to see the salvation brought by Jesus, yet their faith remained strong. Just like Abraham, who set off for an unknown land, we are nomads too, searching for the Kingdom.

Today's Gospel reading begins with the promise of the greatest treasure—the Kingdom of God. Jesus says real treasure is the kind that never wears out. We never have to worry about being robbed. We don't need an armored car or a bank vault to hold this kind of treasure; the best place to store it is in our heart. "'Wherever your treasure lies, there your heart will be.'"

The rest of the Gospel reading calls on us to be ready for God. One example describes wide-awake servants who are well prepared for the master. No thief will break into this house. "'The Son of Man will come when you least expect him.'" Peter didn't quite understand, so Jesus tried again. Once again, servants are used as examples. The busy servant is fortunate. The lazy one, who abused privileges and didn't worry about the master's return, ends up with a beating. "'When much has been given, . . . much will be required.'"

Both the Gospel reading and the first reading urge us to live our life as if Jesus is about to arrive any minute. We must take responsibility for our actions; be ready and be faithful.

Themes for Teens   The following themes from the Scriptures relate to the lives of teens:
- God has chosen us.
- Treasure your faith.
- Will you be ready?
- Don't wait until the last minute.
- Be ready for God.

Our Response

Activity   ### Will You Be Ready?

This reflection is designed to jump-start the teens into thinking about the message found in today's Gospel passage: "'The Son of Man will come when you least expect him.'"

Ask the young people to gather quietly in your chapel area or prayer space. Remind them to remain quiet throughout this reflection.

Place a timer in the middle of the prayer space where all can see it. (If you have a large group, you may want to use several timers so that all the teens can hear the time ticking away as well as see it ticking away.)

Read Luke 12:32–48.

Set the timer for 20 minutes and say:
- Jesus will be here in 20 minutes. How are you going to spend the next 20 minutes?

  After the bell on the timer rings, say:
- "'The Son of Man will come when you least expect him.'" Will you be ready?

Activity Ideas   The following activity ideas also relate to the Scripture readings. You may want to read the passage(s) indicated as part of the activity.

- With their families, ask the teens to create a family treasure chest by decorating a shoe box with copies of family pictures. Then have them read today's second reading. Tell them to have each person in the family write one family blessing, share it with the rest of the family, and place it inside the family treasure chest. Suggest that they take the treasure chest out every couple of months and repeat the activity. (Heb. 11:1–2,8–19)

- Sing "God Has Chosen Me," by Bernadette Farrell (*Today's Missal, Music Issue, 1997,* no. 679), or a similar song. Read the verses from today's psalm in between each verse of the song. (Ps. 33:1,12,18–19)

- Invite the teens to plan a "homecoming weekend" for Jesus. Ask them to think about the following questions before breaking into groups to plan the homecoming:
  ○ Are we as a group, parish, or school ready for the return of the Master?
  ○ What do we need to change?
  ○ How do we think Jesus will return?

  (Luke 12:32–48)

- After reading today's Gospel, ask the teens in small groups to identify some of the symbols found in the reading—little flock, lamps burning ready, purses that never wear out, and so on—and draw them on a poster. Direct the teens to discuss each symbol and to write down next to it what we can learn from it. (Luke 12:32–48)

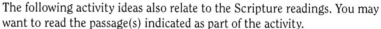

Ordinary Time

Twentieth Sunday of the Year

Scripture Readings (121)

- ❖ Jer. 38:4–6,8–10
- ❖ Ps. 40:2,3,4,18
- ❖ Heb. 12:1–4
- ❖ Luke 12:49–53

God's Word

A major theme of the Scripture readings is "An unpopular race."

Jeremiah was shaking things up. It is, of course, the job of a prophet to get people thinking. Prophets do not always say what people want to hear. In this reading the princes try to do away with Jeremiah. They try to convince the king that Jeremiah's prophesying is getting the people and the soldiers upset and that it will lead to their ruin. Jeremiah will not give up preaching, so Jeremiah's foes throw the prophet into a well where he is up to his nose in mud. But Jeremiah has a champion, Ebed-melech, who gets permission from the king to pull Jeremiah out of the well and rescue him from death.

This psalm is both a lament and a prayer of thanksgiving. We can join Jeremiah and the psalmist by calling out to God in our time of need. Often, this type of prayer—petition—is the most comfortable, because we often reach out to God when we need something. We may not find ourselves literally up to our neck in mud like Jeremiah, but often we feel overwhelmed by personal or family problems. We can feel like we are lost deep in a well. In the psalm, our champion is God, who saves us from affliction and poverty.

The second reading compares following Jesus to the running of a race. We are told that Jesus is at the finish line. We can get discouraged sometimes, but we need to catch our breath and keep running toward Jesus. We need to avoid the obstacle of sin so that nothing weighs us down or trips us up. The race is as important as the goal. We can draw inspiration from Jesus, who suffered much while running the race.

As in Jeremiah, the Gospel reading describes Jesus letting everyone know he hasn't come to leave things the way they are. His message of compassionate outreach to outcasts, tax collectors, and people regarded as sinners does not allow business as usual. This Gospel seems harsh, but being a follower of Jesus is a radical change of life. Jesus and Jeremiah challenged the morals and values of their day. So, too, living like a Christian is not that popular today.

Sharing the Gospel can lead to opposition. Jesus' message sometimes divides families and friends. In this reading, fire is not a destructive symbol but a purifying one. Following Jesus can lead to a baptism by fire, but after we race through the fire, Jesus awaits us on the other side.

Themes for Teens

The following themes from the Scriptures relate to the lives of teens:

- Peace comes at a price.
- Run toward Jesus.
- Call on God when in need.
- God will rescue you.
- Pray for help.

Our Response

Watching Television with Jesus

This journaling exercise is keyed to the Gospel reading. It is designed to get the teens to look critically at the values portrayed on television in light of the values and morals taught by Jesus.

Ask the young people to watch at least five different types of shows on television over a period of a week. Tell them to make sure they leave room next to them on the couch so Jesus has a place to sit.

After they watch each show, direct the teens to answer the following questions in their journal:
- How did you feel about having Jesus watch the show with you?
- What morals or values found in the show conflict with the teachings of Jesus?

At the end of the week, having watched and journaled on five shows, ask the teens to respond to the following in their journal:
- How might you change your viewing habits after watching television with Jesus?
- How might you change your values or attitudes after this exercise?

Activity Ideas

The following activity ideas also relate to the Scripture readings. You may want to read the passage(s) indicated as part of the activity.

- Ask the teens to make a checklist of the equipment and preparations a runner must have and make in order to successfully run a race. Read Heb. 12:1–4. Next, ask the teens to make a checklist of what we need for our race toward Jesus. (Heb. 12:1–4)

- Sponsor a 10K Run for Jesus. The teens can participate in several ways. Some can run. Others can collect pledges. Another group can plan a prayer service for the starting line and another for the finish line. The pledge money collected can be given to the needy in your parish community. (Heb. 12:1–4)

- Find out if a local camp, ROTC program, or university physical education department has a "wall" station as part of a teamwork-building obstacle course. The station consists of a high, flat, smooth wall. The object of the station is to get a team of eight to ten people over the wall using only one another, cooperation, and teamwork. Call the bottom of the wall the well that Jeremiah was tossed into in the first reading today. After the group successfully gets everyone over the wall, talk about how we need to work together to help one another out of the "wells" in our life. (Jer. 38:4–6, 8–10; Ps. 40:2,3,4,18)

- Invite a counselor from the local Catholic Charities organization to raise awareness in the teens about the signs of depression. This can help teens recognize depression in themselves and seek help, or get help for a friend who is hurting. Close with a prayer—held in the dark—asking God to rescue all of us from the darkness in our life. (Jer. 38:4–6,8–10; Ps. 40:2,3,4,18)

Ordinary Time

Twenty-first Sunday of the Year

Scripture Readings (124)

- ❖ Isa. 66:18–21
- ❖ Ps. 117:1–2
- ❖ Heb. 12:5–7,11–13
- ❖ Luke 13:22–30

God's Word

A major theme of the Scripture readings is "Entering the Kingdom."

The first reading from Isaiah proclaims that the Good News is for all people in all countries. It does not matter what language they speak or where they live. God is speaking to them—and to us. Missionaries are sent out to proclaim the Good News and to call people of all nations to join them in Israel, the holy place of God's dwelling.

The psalm also calls on us to share the message of God with all people. It includes a promise that the Lord will stay with us always, and it states that we are to praise and honor our God.

The second reading is a lesson in discipline. No one likes to follow rules. No one likes to be punished. But the writer of today's passage knows that parents discipline us because they love us. So, too, God sets rules for us to live by. We are all still in training for the race (mentioned in last week's readings), and we need to build up our arms and legs. We are told to make straight our path—or perhaps to clean up our act.

The Gospel reading tells how Jesus traveled to Jerusalem. Many people ask how to be saved and enter God's Kingdom. There is no easy answer. Jesus uses the example of the narrow door to describe how difficult it might be to enter the Kingdom. We want to enter the Kingdom on our own terms, but it is up to God to decide. Jesus *is* the narrow door that leads to the Kingdom, and we need to walk with Jesus. As in the first reading, salvation is offered to all, but some choose to reject it. Those who hear the word of God and respond will be invited to the feast.

Once again, Jesus turns the normal way of looking at things upside down. The "'last will be first and . . . [the] first will be last.'" Those who think they hold the keys to the kingdom might be left standing outside a locked door.

Themes for Teens

The following themes from the Scriptures relate to the lives of teens:
- Open the doors of the Kingdom.
- Be ready for the Kingdom.
- Share the Good News.
- Discipline can be good.
- Get on the straight path.

Our Response

Activity   Passwords and Mazes

These icebreakers are designed to help spark discussion on the imagery found in today's Gospel and to help teens think about ways to avoid the obstacles and "locked doors" on our journey toward the Kingdom.

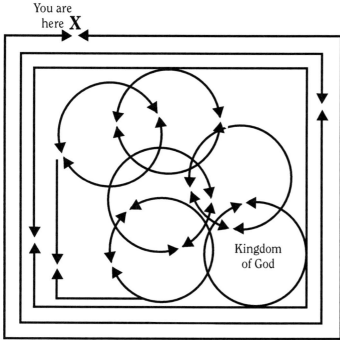

You are here **X**

Kingdom of God

- When the teens arrive, make sure the door to their regular meeting place is locked. A sign on the door should say, "Knock if you want to come in, and give the password." Begin your meeting on the Kingdom of God by asking the teens what they think the password is for entering the Kingdom.
- As another icebreaker, give the young people a copy of the maze shown below. Direct them to find the Kingdom of God at the end of the maze. Ask the teens to identify some obstacles along the way, and have them write them on the maze. Then share in small groups.

  Close with a short prayer asking God to help the teens overcome the obstacles in the way on the journey toward the Kingdom.

Activity Ideas

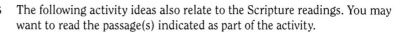

The following activity ideas also relate to the Scripture readings. You may want to read the passage(s) indicated as part of the activity.

- Invite a missionary to speak to the teens about his or her experiences—and about how teens can help. Or adopt a youth group from another country and establish a pen-pal relationship of fellowship and evangelization. (Isa. 66:18–21; Ps. 117:1–2)

- Invite the teens to trade places with their parents in role-plays about discipline and setting rules. Ask them the following questions:
  - What rules would you set for your own children? as five-year-olds? as ten-year-olds? as fifteen-year-olds?
  - Why would you set these rules?
  - Why are rules important?
  - What are some of the rules God asks us to live by?

    (Heb. 12:5–7,11–13)

- Challenge the teens to write a prayer service with the theme "Keys to the Kingdom." They could compose prayers of petition asking God to help us get through the locked door. A large set of janitor's keys or a ring of plastic infant keys could be used as a symbol, with the rest of the prayer service being built around them. (Luke 13:22–30)

- Give each teen a membership card to the Kingdom of God. Ask the teens what they are going to do to keep their membership from expiring. Urge them to keep the card in their wallet or purse as a reminder of the promise of the Kingdom of Heaven. (Luke 13:22–30)

Ordinary Time

Twenty-second Sunday of the Year

Scripture Readings (127)

- ❖ Sir. 3:17–18,20,28–29
- ❖ Ps. 68:4–5,6–7,10–11
- ❖ Heb. 12:18–19,22–24
- ❖ Luke 14:1,7–14

God's Word

A major theme of the Scripture readings is "Be humble of heart."

Humility is one of the favorite topics of the writers of wisdom literature. This passage reads a little like a parent telling a child how to behave around others. A lesson on the value of humility is needed as much today as in the time of Sirach. The first meaning of humility is to recognize our proper place before God and before one another. All are of unique value in the eyes of God. This is easy to forget in a very competitive culture where first is best. The gift of humility is far more valuable than material things.

In the psalm we see how God sets priorities. Poor people, orphans, and prisoners come first. Those who are considered last in society take a place at the head of God's table. In God's Kingdom no one is homeless. God has made a "home for the poor."

The Letter to the Hebrews contrasts the Covenant of God and Moses at Sinai with the New Covenant of God in Jesus and the promise of eternal life. The writer of Hebrews tries to bolster the faith of the reader with a picture of an intimate God drawing near to us. God is not unapproachable and untouchable.

The Gospel of Luke tells a story about going to a banquet. Jesus decides on this parable when the invited guests start vying for the best places at the table, and he can see a lesson on humility is in order.

Not only does the story tell the disciples to take the worst seat at the table, but it also gives advice about who to invite to the table. As in the psalm, Jesus sets a place at the table for the poor, the crippled, and the needy.

We also should not seek any repayment for our humility. God isn't just talking about a dinner party, but about the Kingdom of God, where "'everyone who exalts himself shall be humbled and he who humbles himself shall be exalted.'"

The big shots, the greedy rich people, and those who are ambitious for honors are so busy worrying about who sits where, who gets ahead first, that they have no time to listen to God's word. The poor and the outcasts know that they need God.

From these readings we learn, first, that the poor are closest to God and, second, that as disciples we must live in humility with others and God instead of simply for ourselves.

Themes for Teens

The following themes from the Scriptures relate to the lives of teens:
- Being humble is more valuable than gifts.
- The poor come first with God.
- God is at home with the poor.
- The poor come home to God.
- Don't sit in the best seat.

Our Response

Activity

The First Will Be Last

This icebreaker focuses on the Gospel reading. It sets up a situation similar to the one the Pharisees found themselves in at the dinner in today's Gospel. It serves as a springboard for discussion about our place at the table in God's Kingdom.

Before the meeting, set up a table with two kinds of drinks, Kool-Aid and soda; along with two snacks, plain crackers and candy bars. If you have thirty teens, make sure you have only five candy bars and lots of plain crackers. Put out only a few cans of soda, with the rest being Kool-Aid. Make sure the teens see the snack table when they arrive for the meeting and know what is on it.

Before discussing today's Gospel, have the teens line up for a snack break, but do not give specific instructions on which group should go first or on how the teens should line up. Watch for any pushing or shoving or running to be at the head of the line. After all have lined up, ask the last five teens to come up to the front of the line. See how the others react.

After the snack, read the Gospel together and talk about the teens' reaction to snacktime and discuss what Jesus is trying to teach about humility.

Activity Ideas

The following activity ideas also relate to the Scripture readings. You may want to read the passage(s) indicated as part of the activity.

- Give each teen some white paper and crayons. Ask the teens to imagine what God's table would look like and to draw it. After reading today's Gospel, ask: "Where do the rich sit? Where do the poor sit? Where do you sit?" (Luke 14:25–33)

- Pray today's psalm together as a family. Talk about what God's home must look like. Discuss ways your family can help God make a home for the poor, then follow through on your family outreach effort. (Ps. 90:3–4,5–6, 12–13,14–17)

- Before your meeting, ask each teen to find a picture or image of God. Hang the pictures on a wall or bulletin board as the young people arrive. Direct a teen to read today's second reading. Encourage the teens to identify images of God from the reading and compare them to the pictures they found. Discuss how our image of God has an effect on how we approach God in prayer. (Heb. 12:18–19,22–24)

- Tell the teens that they are each going to throw a party and they can invite anyone they want. Instruct them to make a guest list with the names of people they will invite. Ask why they invited the people on the list. Also ask who is not on the list and why. In discussing today's Gospel, encourage the young people to be more inclusive and less exclusive in their gatherings. Urge them to find ways to make newcomers, especially, feel welcome. (Luke 14:25–33)

Ordinary Time

Twenty-third Sunday of the Year

Scripture Readings (130)

- ❖ Wis. 9:13–18
- ❖ Ps. 90:3–4,5–6,12–13,14–17
- ❖ Philem. 9–10,12–17
- ❖ Luke 14:25–33

God's Word

A major theme of the Scripture readings is "Words of wisdom."

The writer of this first reading is struck with the awesomeness of God and asks: How can we know what God is up to? So many years after this was written, we ask the same question. The tough part is that we cannot know all the answers. Yet we are not without guidance. Wisdom comes from God. We may not know all the answers, but if we seek the wisdom of God—through prayer, through reading the Scriptures, and through others we meet—we can learn to walk the straight paths.

How comforting to know we can always seek refuge in God. Through every age—from the time of the psalmists to the time when Jesus walked on earth to now—we can count on God as protector. We always have a shelter, a refuge from all the tough challenges we face in our life. But it is a refuge, not an escape. Faith in God is not an excuse to run from the tough times in life, rather faith gives us strength to face them.

This letter from Paul to Philemon is about a runaway slave named Onesimus. Philemon, as was common even for Christians at that time, kept slaves. One runs away and seeks refuge with Paul. While there, the slave becomes a Christian. Paul asks that Philemon not punish the slave, but actually accept him as a brother, a fellow Christian. Philemon is asked to give up his right to punish Onesimus and to possibly face ridicule from neighbors and relatives. This letter really is a radical call to discipleship.

The Gospel reading tells us that Jesus, too, is asking for a different mindset. In case they did not hear it the first time, Jesus emphasizes his requirement that all prospective followers be single-minded in their commitment to follow him. Nothing must come in the way—neither family ties nor possessions.

Jesus gives two examples of the dedication needed to be a disciple: Do not build a tower if you don't have enough money to complete it, and do not go into battle if your army is too small to defeat the enemy.

Strangely enough, Jesus is telling us that the best way to prepare for the journey is to *not* take anything with us—to leave everything behind. Discipleship is not a temporary membership in a club, it is a lifelong commitment.

Themes for Teens

The following themes from the Scriptures relate to the lives of teens:

- Get it straight with God.
- God is our shelter.
- Carry the cross with Jesus.
- Leave everything behind.
- Make a commitment to Jesus.

Our Response

Activity   **Prayer with Empty Pockets**

This meditation, keyed to the Gospel reading, invites the teens to reflect on Jesus' challenge to prevent materialism from being an obstacle to discipleship.

Tell the young people to take everything out of their pockets and place the items in a small pile in front of them.

Proclaim today's Gospel reading.

Ask the teens to choose one of the objects from their pockets and to offer a prayer asking Jesus for the courage and the strength to live more closely as a disciple and to set aside worries about material things.

Here are some examples:
- *Coin.* Dear God, please help me to value your word more than money.
- *Pen.* Dear God, please help me to proclaim your word in my speech and writing.
- *Tissue.* Dear God, please help me to comfort those who are suffering.

Activity Ideas

The following activity ideas also relate to the Scripture readings. You may want to read the passage(s) indicated as part of the activity.

- Invite the teens to interview different family members, especially grandparents, for "words of wisdom" to live by. They might want to record the ideas on a cassette tape to share with other family members, or write them in their journal. (Wis. 9:13–18)

- For a combination Scripture study, outreach, and fund-raiser, challenge the teens to design their own line of greeting cards that highlight words of wisdom from Jesus found in the Scriptures. (All readings)

- Give the young people instructions on how to pitch a tent. Divide them into teams and have a contest to see who can pitch a tent the quickest. Afterward, sit inside a tent and read today's psalm. Discuss the question, "How has God been a shelter or refuge for you?" (Ps. 90:3–4,5–6,12–13, 14–17)

- After reading the Gospel, ask the teens to think of some modern examples of the dedication needed to be a disciple instead of a tower builder and battle planner. Some examples:
  ○ Would you fly a plane without filling it with fuel and filing a flight plan?
  ○ Would you take your final exams without studying for more than a minute?

(Luke 14:25–33)

Twenty-fourth Sunday of the Year

Scripture Readings (133)

- ❖ Exod. 32:7–11,13–14
- ❖ Ps. 51:3–4,12–13,17,19
- ❖ 1 Tim. 1:12–17
- ❖ Luke 15:1–32

God's Word

A major theme of the Scripture readings is "Stories of God's mercy."

Today's first reading is part of the story of the Israelites' trek through the desert. Despite all the good things God has done for them, the Israelites build their own golden calf idol and worship it. God tells Moses he is fed up with these wayward people and will unleash wrath upon them. Moses, used to appealing to God for these stubborn people, asks God to reconsider. Calling on God's compassion, Moses recalls with God the promises God made to Abraham and Isaac. God keeps these promises and forgives the people their sins.

The refrain in today's psalm foreshadows the change of heart we will read about in the Gospel. We pray to turn away from the path of sin and to receive a new heart and spirit true to God. "I . . . go to my father" reminds us that prayer is an action. We go to God when we are in need. God, as father, is approachable, someone we can lean on. The psalmist asks for cleansing, to have all guilt washed away so that only a clean heart remains.

The author of the First Letter to Timothy writes in Paul's name and reflects on a sinful life of persecuting Christians, and recalls how Jesus had mercy on him, a sinner. The writer tells his own story of sin and forgiveness to give hope to others that they will find forgiveness in Jesus Christ. In the first reading, the patience of God is shown through Moses. Here, God's forgiving love is found in Jesus Christ. "Christ came to save sinners."

In the Gospel reading, Jesus tells three stories to the Pharisees—and to us—so that they—and we—might better understand God's forgiveness. The first is a shortened version of the parable of the lost sheep. A shepherd with one hundred sheep loses one and searches and searches until it is found. So, too, God searches for the lost sheep and rejoices in the sinner who returns to the fold.

The second parable is about a woman who searches by lamplight for a lost coin. Though we may often feel insignificant—like a single lost coin—God, like the woman, celebrates when we are found.

The third story is the parable of the prodigal son. A son squanders the family wealth and lives a sinful life while the older brother toils away. When the wayward son comes to his senses, he returns home to the open arms of his dad. The prodigal asks for forgiveness and is forgiven. When the other son is stunned and appalled, the father invites him to the celebration and asks that all be forgiven.

All of the readings today ask us to recognize our sins, give them up, and return to God. There we will find forgiveness and joy. No matter where we go or how we are lost, we can always come home.

Themes for Teens The following themes from the Scriptures relate to the lives of teens:
- The lost will be found.
- God keeps his promises.
- God will forgive you.
- Jesus came to save us.
- We can always come home.

Our Response

Activity **The Prodigal Daughter**

This adaptation of one of today's Gospel parables encourages the young people to find the connection between Jesus' teaching and the need for forgiveness in their own life.

Ask one of the teens to read "The Prodigal Daughter," by Lisa-Marie Calderone-Stewart:

> Once upon a time, there was a single mother living with her daughter and son. They were a close and happy family, and they got along for the most part, although they did fight now and then.
>
> One day, after the daughter had graduated from high school, she went to her mother and said, "I'm eighteen and I'm old enough to be on my own. Please give me all the money we have saved up for my college tuition. I want to travel and see the world, get a job, and start living in a new and exciting place."
>
> The mother was sad. She tried to convince her daughter to stay home with the family and go to a local college, but the daughter refused. So the mother gave her the money and said good-bye.
>
> The daughter went to a big city and rented an apartment. She made a lot of friends and went out to eat every night. She was having so much fun that she kept forgetting to look for a job. Eventually, she ran out of money, and she was kicked out of her apartment. The daughter found out that it wasn't easy to get a job. So she just walked the streets, eating whatever food she could find in the dumpsters behind the restaurants where she used to be a customer. And nobody seemed to recognize her, and no one wanted to help her.
>
> The daughter finally decided to go back home and ask her mother to hire her as a housekeeper. She figured she could cook, clean, and take care of the house, because she could never ask to return home as a real daughter—not after wasting all that money.
>
> So the daughter returned home. Her mother was so happy to see her that she threw her arms around her and kissed her dirty face, brought her in, and poured her a cup of hot chocolate. The mother called for her son to come downstairs to celebrate. Then she called all her friends and relatives and told them to come over right away because her daughter had come back.
>
> The daughter couldn't believe all this attention! She got hugs and kisses and presents from all her aunts and uncles and cousins that she hadn't seen for a long time.
>
> Eventually, the mother realized her son had not come downstairs from his bedroom. She went up to get him.
>
> The son was furious. He started screaming at his mother so loudly that everyone downstairs heard him: "How could you do this? How could you reward her after she wasted all the money you saved up for her college education? She never even got a job! Look at her! She's a mess! I'm

embarrassed to be her brother. I've been here all along; I get the good grades; I have a part-time job; I help you around the house; and you never gave me a party! That's why I'm not coming down to her stupid party."

The mother pleaded with him. "You are my only son, and I have enjoyed living with you all these years. You are wonderful, and I am so thankful that you have been with me. But no matter how angry you are at your sister, she is still your sister. And even if she used up all her money, she is still alive! It's been so long since we've seen her, I thought she was dead! So I'm excited that she's back. You haven't even said hello to her. Please come downstairs and join us." (*Faith Works for Junior High,* pp. 70–71)

Allow a few minutes of quiet time. Close with a prayer for all children and parents who are separated by misunderstanding or a lack of forgiveness, that God will help them find a way beyond their differences and bring them back together again.

Activity Ideas

The following activity ideas also relate to the Scripture readings. You may want to read the passage(s) indicated as part of the activity.

- Ask the teens to respond to the following statements and questions in their journal:
  - Reflect on a time when you felt like a lost sheep or a lost coin, a lost daughter or son.
  - Recall a time when you were lost as a child—separated from your parents for even a short time. How did it feel to be lost? How did it feel when you were reunited with your family?
  - Write about a time when someone forgave you. How did you experience God's love through this person?

(All readings)

- As an icebreaker, divide the teens into teams and give them 5 minutes to brainstorm and write down as many slogans or sayings as they can think of that include the word *home.* Examples: "Home is where the heart is," "there's no place like home," "home away from home," "home, sweet home," and so on. Use this as a starting point to reflect on today's readings and on how our forgiving God always welcomes us home. (All readings)

- Locate the lost-and-found box or closet in your school or parish. Invite the teens to look through the contents. Challenge them to write a story from the point of view of a lost item—an old umbrella, a lost jacket, or the like. After the teens have had fun sharing their imaginary stories, direct them to reflect quietly on this question: What stories are in your personal lost-and-found box? (Luke 15:1–32)

- Invite the teens to write their own penance service using the three stories found in today's Gospel. After reading the parable of the lost sheep, ask the teens to write two examination of conscience questions and a prayer of forgiveness or an act of contrition based on the story. They can do the same for the parables of the lost coin and the prodigal son. If possible, offer the teens a chance to receive the sacrament of reconciliation. (Luke 15:1–32)

Twenty-fifth Sunday of the Year

Scripture Readings (136)

❖ Amos 8:4–7
❖ Ps. 113:1–2,4–6,7–8
❖ 1 Tim. 2:1–8
❖ Luke 16:1–13

God's Word

A major theme of the Scripture readings is "Be good stewards."

The first reading from Amos—who is often called the prophet of social justice—is a warning to people who trample on others to get ahead, those who profit by taking advantage of other people. This reading deals with the buying and selling of grain. It was a practice to fix the scales so that poor people paid more or received less. These dealers also saw the Sabbath as an inconvenience to their business. Instead of seeing it as a time set aside for God, they grumbled about the business loss. Amos is a good steward for speaking out against injustice. In today's world, cheating by fixing a scale seems so insignificant compared to modern ways of using and abusing others—especially helpless people.

The psalmist tells us that God is the champion of poor people. While others put them down, God lifts them up. This psalm recalls the Gospel of a few weeks ago in which Jesus says that the first will be last and the last will be first. Here we are assured that poor people will sit with princes in the Kingdom of Heaven.

The second reading calls on us to pray for everyone, even the leaders in our world. Our prayers can help them make the right decisions on how to use the money and resources entrusted to them. Our prayer should include all people, because God wishes everyone to be saved. The writer of this letter also tells us that Jesus is the mediator between God and us. We are able to grow closer to God through Jesus, especially as Jesus teaches us how to pray to God.

Today's Gospel reading is about the use of resources, about using what God has given us to help others. The parable starts with a manager who is called to give an accounting to the boss. Afraid of getting fired, the manager plays *Let's Make a Deal* with the master's debtors and ends up ahead. The parable suggests that we use the things of this world in such a way that when they are no longer of any worth to us, we will have built an account with God that offers a lasting reception.

The last part of this Gospel holds the warning that we cannot serve two masters—God and money. One must lose out. The meaning money holds for us can reveal the type of person we are. We are called to serve God and to make good use of money, to be good stewards of what God has given us.

Themes for Teens

The following themes from the Scriptures relate to the lives of teens:
• God champions the poor.
• Use your gifts for others.
• Pray for all leaders.
• Serve God, not money.
• You are gifted.

Ordinary Time

Our Response

Activity   Being Good Stewards of Money

This discussion and role-play activity is keyed to the Gospel reading. It asks the young people to think about the way they use money. The teens are asked to make some choices and to talk through their decisions.

Ask the teens to reflect on these questions: "What is the role of money in your life at the present? What will it be in the future?"

Divide the teens into groups of four to six, and give each group a set of the following questions or situations:

- Would you go back to a store if you discovered someone gave you the wrong change?
- If your parents have the money to pay for your college costs, what reasons are there to save for it yourself?
- What purchases can be considered examples of exercising good stewardship of money? What purchases show poor stewardship of money?

After discussing these questions, ask the teens to come up with their own questions to challenge the others.

Close by asking the teens to reflect on the question, "How do we harm ourselves as well as others when we are poor stewards of our money?"

Activity Ideas

The following activity ideas also relate to the Scripture readings. You may want to read the passage(s) indicated as part of the activity.

- Sing the song "The Cry of the Poor," by John Foley (*Glory and Praise*, vol. 2 [Phoenix, AZ: North American Liturgy Resources, 1982], no. 93). Between each verse, ask the teens to offer a prayer of petition asking God's help for someone in need who is close to home or far away. (Amos 8:4–7; Ps. 113:1–2,4–6,7–8)

- Invite the teens to do this self-affirmation in order to recognize their gifts and consider ways to use them more wisely for others. Ask the teens to cover shoe boxes with white paper and top them with a gift bow. With markers, have them write some of their own gifts and talents on the box, highlighting two that they would like to share more with others. After discussion with a partner, ask the teens to take their boxes home and put them in their room as a reminder to use the gifts God has given them. (Luke 16:1–13)

- If the prophet Amos were alive today, what injustices in our world would he point out? After proclaiming the first reading, ask the teens to use the TV news or a newspaper as a starting point to identify these areas of concern. (Amos 8:4–7)

- As the second reading reminds us, prayers are not only for our family and friends but for our leaders as well. Help the teens list our elected officials—from the president of the United States to senators, members of congress, state representatives, and city or local officials. Divide the teens into pairs to write petitions. Pass them along to the person in your parish who prepares the petitions for Mass so that some can be used in the next few weeks. (1 Tim. 2:1–8)

Twenty-sixth Sunday of the Year

Scripture Readings (139)

- ❖ Amos 6:1,4–7
- ❖ Ps. 146:7,8–9,9–10
- ❖ 1 Tim. 6:11–16
- ❖ Luke 16:19–31

God's Word

A major theme of the Scripture readings is "Lasting wealth."

These readings continue a theme of compassion for the poor and contain a harsh warning for those who feast while others starve.

In the first reading, Amos points out the excesses of the Israelites. The prophet continues to rebuke the "haves" for the way they treat the "have-nots." The haves are the people who eat the best food and lounge around all day. They are the couch potatoes of the Hebrew Scriptures—only these couches are beds of ivory. The prophet warns that all this lavish living has a price, and that in the end they will lose all they have in exile.

The psalmist praises God for being just and for making the oppressed rejoice. Whether hungry or impoverished or a stranger, "the Lord raises up those that [are] bowed down," a theme that echoes last week's readings. We are called to model God's concern for the poor if we are to live as Christians.

The First Letter to Timothy is a pep talk for Christians. "Fight the good fight of faith" sounds a little like a cheer. The writer urges us to seek piety, faith, integrity, and a gentle spirit. We are asked to recall our profession of faith and to hold onto it. The reading closes with a psalm of praise and glory to God.

Today's Gospel story, found only in the Gospel of Luke, contrasts the life, death, and reward of two people—a rich man who lived it up, and a poor beggar who was sick and hungry. The rich man is given no name in this passage, but in Greek the beggar's name, Lazarus, is translated "my God helps." After death, Lazarus rests with Abraham while the rich man suffers torment.

The rich man—who never sought to aid Lazarus—asks for comforting water to be brought to him. But Abraham says that the rich man got what he deserved. Perhaps thinking about someone else for the first time, the former rich man asks that his brothers be warned so that they will not suffer the same fate. Abraham tells him no. They have the prophets to listen to.

Themes for Teens

The following themes from the Scriptures relate to the lives of teens:
- Fast living fades away.
- Keep the faith.
- Help the have-nots.
- Reach out to others.
- Don't wait until it is too late.

Ordinary Time

Our Response

Activity

A Bowl of Rice

This activity is keyed to the readings as a whole. It helps raise the young peoples' awareness of the hungry in our world, and it challenges them to make a small effort to help those in need. You may want to do this activity with your group at lunch or dinner.

Ask the teens to write down everything they ate the day before. Next, in the center of your meeting place, put a typical fast-food meal—burger, fries, and a Coke—on one side of the table, and a small bowl of rice on the other side.

Ask the teens to reflect on the following:

> The rice in this bowl is all some people have had to eat today, some perhaps even less. Not only do we fail to appreciate the abundance of food we have, we often waste it.

Ask someone from a local Red Cross or Christian relief organization to talk about her or his experience with the poor in other countries and to engage the teens in talking about what they can do to help the poor, especially the hungry.

Contact the organizers of Operation Rice Bowl and invite the teens to participate in this effort that combines prayer for the needy with fasting and almsgiving. Many parishes consider doing this during Lent. Why not do it at a different time of the year? UNICEF is another worthy cause that specifically targets needy children. The young people could participate individually or as a group.

Activity Ideas

The following activity ideas also relate to the Scripture readings. You may want to read the passage(s) indicated as part of the activity.

- Do you throw out food you haven't eaten? Ask the teens to stand by a trash can in the school cafeteria one day and write in their journal what they discover.
  - How much food was thrown out?
  - How does this relate to today's readings?
  - What can we do to avoid waste in our own eating habits?

  (All readings)

    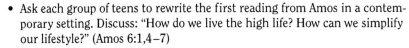

- Ask each group of teens to rewrite the first reading from Amos in a contemporary setting. Discuss: "How do we live the high life? How can we simplify our lifestyle?" (Amos 6:1,4–7)

- After reading today's psalm, ask the teens to give examples of people who are oppressed, hungry, captive, blind, strangers, homeless. Urge them to give examples not only of people they have read about in the newspaper but also of people they know in their own community. Help them to put real faces on these problems. Ask each teen to think of one way he or she can make a difference in these areas of need. (Ps. 146:7,8–9,9–10)

- Ask the teens to search the Scriptures for other occasions when Jesus teaches about social justice and the responsibility of Christians to reach out to others. Create a poster together with the headings "God's Word" and "Our Response" written on it. Under "God's Word," write the Scripture citation, and under "Our Response," write the way we are called to live in response to God's challenge to justice. (All readings)

Twenty-seventh Sunday of the Year

Scripture Readings (142)
- ❖ Hab. 1:2–3; 2:2–4
- ❖ Ps. 95:1–2,6–7,8–9
- ❖ 2 Tim. 1:6–8,13–14
- ❖ Luke 17:5–10

God's Word

A major theme of the Scripture readings is "A faith that serves."

The writer of today's first reading struggles with unanswered prayers. Perhaps a victim of violence, Habakkuk lives in a time when human rights are regularly violated and the poor are oppressed. Habakkuk is asking, "Why do the evil win and the just lose out?" Habakkuk's culture of injustice seems similar to our culture. Eventually, the Lord hears the prayers of Habakkuk and speaks in a vision. God promises to act with justice and mercy, but calls on upright people to persevere in faith through these tough times.

If today you heard God's voice, what would you do? The psalmist invites us to be open to the word of God, to approach God with open hands and heart. It is easy to be doubtful and cynical in this world. Believers are often met with scorn. The psalmist seeks another response—to sing joyfully, to be thankful. The image of the shepherd is key here. We are asked to show reverence in word and action—to worship God and to kneel in respect.

While the psalmist asks us to listen to the voice of God, the author of the second reading urges us to not be ashamed of what we believe. It is okay to be proud to be a Christian. We cannot just keep the faith, we need to live it. The Spirit will give us courage to use our gifts to serve God and others. Living the Gospel is difficult, but we can be sure of the wisdom and love that make us strong.

In the Gospel of Luke, Jesus tells the disciples that even small amounts of faith can be powerful. He tells two stories. In the first story, Jesus says that faith the size of a tiny mustard seed has the power to uproot an entire tree. So, too, faith has the power to radically change our life and the lives of all who come in contact with us. The second story highlights the call for Christians to serve one another with humility, never requiring recognition or return payment. Disciples receive no winning lottery ticket, no A on a report card, and seldom a thank-you card. Jesus is not trying to discourage his disciples, but he warns them away from seeking personal glory. A good servant is happy with serving for the sake of serving and seeks nothing more.

It is the quality of faith, not the quantity, that is important. Faith calls us to service, and service serves to strengthen our faith.

Themes for Teens

The following themes from the Scriptures relate to the lives of teens:
- Be open to God's voice.
- Listen with your heart.
- Faith is a powerful gift.
- Serve God, not yourself.
- Faith is powerful.

Ordinary Time

Our Response

Activity | **If I Only Had Some Courage**

This activity is keyed to the second reading and the Gospel. It uses examples from a classic video to help the young people recognize that they have the faith to be Christians and the courage to share their faith.

Show the first video clip from the classic movie *The Wizard of Oz*. The scene opens with Dorothy meeting the cowardly lion. The lion tells her about his quest to find some courage. The scene ends as they continue their journey down the yellow brick road.

Direct the teens to read today's Gospel together in pairs. The lion in *The Wizard of Oz* is afraid he does not have enough courage. The disciples' request for more faith is similar to the lion's quest for courage. Ask the pairs to discuss the following questions:

• In what areas of your life do you lack courage?
• Why does it take courage to live like a Christian today?

Show the scene in the video where the lion approaches the wizard and learns that he had courage all along and did not realize it. The disciples, too, already had faith. They were followers of Jesus. They just didn't realize that they had more than enough faith.

Have each pair join another to make a foursome. Discuss:

• How can we support each other in our faith?
• How can we find courage to share our faith?
• How does faith lead to service?

Show the video clip where Dorothy affirms the courage the lion now realizes. Affirming others of their strength and talents is a real service.

Ask the whole group to note ways they have been affirmed by others and what that meant to them.

You may want to give each teen a homemade prayer card with a lion sticker and this prayer: "God, give me the courage to share my faith by being of service to others."

Activity Ideas | The following activity ideas also relate to the Scripture readings. You may want to read the passage(s) indicated as part of the activity.

• Borrow barbells or weights from someone in your parish who lifts weights. Gather the teens in a circle around the weights, and ask a volunteer to lift all the weights by himself or herself. Make sure the task is impossible, but take care to avoid injury. Ask the group how the teen might accomplish the task. The answer is, of course, with help from others. Close by talking about how God often gives us the strength we need through other people. (2 Tim. 1:6–8,13–14)

• After sharing the first reading, invite the teens to pray for victims of human rights abuses around the world. If you want more than local newspapers as a source, you may want to contact Amnesty International, a group that works worldwide to advocate for those who struggle for freedom. (Hab. 1:2–3; 2:2–4)

• Identify opportunities for service in your parish or school. You may even want representatives of helping ministries to tell the teens more about what they do. Considering today's Gospel, talk about the motivations to serve. Without setting a quota for a number of hours, ask the teens to do some service in the next two weeks. Later, regather the teens and have them share their experiences of serving others and then answer this question: "How did God speak to your heart through this act of service?" (All readings)

- If today you heard God's voice, what would you do? After reflecting on today's readings, invite the teens to answer the following questions in their journal:
  - ○ Jesus often speaks to us through other people. Who are some of the people today who speak for and with the voice of God?
  - ○ How do other people react to these mouthpieces of God?
  - ○ What causes people to react with hard hearts?
  - ○ What can we do to soften hearts to the word of God?

(Hab. 1:2–3; 2:2–4; Ps. 95:1–2,6–7,8–9)

Twenty-eighth Sunday of the Year

**Scripture Readings
(145)**

- ❖ 2 Kings 5:14–17
- ❖ Ps. 98:1,2–3,3–4
- ❖ 2 Tim. 2:8–13
- ❖ Luke 17:11–19

God's Word

A major theme of the Scripture readings is "Faith saves."

People suffering from leprosy have key roles in today's first reading and in the Gospel reading. Rarely seen today, this terrible disease cripples the body and spirit, disfiguring people and making them outcasts, abandoned by all.

The author of the Second Book of Kings tells of the healing of Naaman, an army officer suffering from leprosy. He goes to the prophet Elisha who tells Naaman to take seven baths in the river Jordan. Naaman is cured physically and finds faith in God. The cure helps the officer see the power of God. Elisha won't take any gifts from Naaman for the cure, saying that only God working through the prophet can do such great things. Naaman proclaims that there is only God and promises to worship none other.

The responsorial is the beginning of Psalm 98. It celebrates the saving power of God and the way God reveals our salvation. The "right hand" mentioned in the first verse refers to God as the champion of justice. God does not save just a few but all nations; not just Israel but to the ends of the earth. No matter who we are or where our life takes us, God will save us.

The Second Letter to Timothy is a lesson in perseverance, a plea to hang in there through the rough times. We are promised that we will live with Jesus in the end. Paul explains how living and speaking as a follower of Christ led to a prison term. Yet the disciple accepts suffering as part of being a Christian and says that physical chains or prison bars cannot chain the word of God. The reading starts with a proclamation at the center of our faith—the Resurrection. Paul tells Timothy that those who suffer for Jesus' sake will be rewarded. We cannot be fair-weather Christians, only believing when it is comfortable or fashionable. We cannot believe in God only when it feels good. As we stick with God, so, too, God sticks with us.

The Gospel of Luke tells how Jesus, continuing on the journey to Jerusalem, encounters ten lepers. They ask for pity and are bewildered when Jesus sends them to the priests. They are not cured in the presence of Jesus,

Ordinary Time

but on the journey. When one of them realizes what has happened, he cannot contain himself. He tells everyone what has happened and rushes back to Jesus to say thank-you. No one knows what happened to the other nine, but Jesus notices that they are missing. Jesus also notes that the one who returned was a Samaritan, a foreigner. Once again, Jesus ties the need for physical healing to the need for spiritual healing: "'Your faith has been your salvation.'"

Jesus calls the lepers out of their shame and isolation and returns them to the community. Jesus gives faces to the lepers; they become real people. The same happens when Jesus rescues us from our sins. All these readings calling for gratitude highlight the difference between simply being healed of a physical disease and being saved.

Themes for Teens The following themes from the Scriptures relate to the lives of teens:
- There is only one God.
- God saves.
- Hang in there with God.
- God sticks with us.
- Thank God!

Our Response

Activity   I Thank You, God, For . . .

These journal prayers are keyed to the first reading and the Gospel. They urge the young people to reflect on the great gifts God has given us and to expand their repertoire of prayer from simple petitions to prayers of thanksgiving.

In their journals, ask the teens to list ten things, people, or gifts that they are thankful for. Some examples can include physical things God has given us—like food to eat or a roof over our head; important people in our life—close friends or family members; or a talent God has given us—such as a musical or writing talent or a skill for playing ice hockey or for fixing computers.

Sometimes it comes more naturally to ask God for things than to thank God in prayer. Have you ever thanked God for any of the things that you've listed in your journal? Over the next ten days, invite the teens to write a prayer each day in their journal, thanking God for each of their gifts.

Activity Ideas The following activity ideas also relate to the Scripture readings. You may want to read the passage(s) indicated as part of the activity.

- AIDS has often been called the leprosy of today's society. Its victims are shunned and suffer discrimination. Invite someone from your community who works with AIDS patients to answer the young people's questions about the disease. Or ask the teens to do some research to find out how the local community and churches help victims of the disease, and what the teens can do to help. Wearing red ribbons just isn't enough. (2 Kings 5:14–17; Luke 17:11–19)

- Ask the teens to think of a time when they should have said thank-you and didn't, or of a time when they should have written a thank-you note but they didn't, or of a person in their life whom they take for granted and need to thank. In light of today's Gospel, urge them to go back now and say thank-you. (Luke 17:11–19)

- On large strips of paper, write down some of the forces of evil in our world that try to silence or diminish the word of God. Then share them with the group. Link all the strips together in a chain and encircle the entire group with it. After sharing today's second reading, invite the teens to respond, "There is no chaining the word of God." Then have them break through the chain around them. (2 Tim. 2:8–13)

• The psalm proclaims that the Lord has revealed to the nations his saving power. Give the teens copies of the Christian Testament and ask them to do a Scripture search in Luke's Gospel for ways Jesus revealed his identity on his journey to Jerusalem. (Ps. 98:1,2–3,3–4)

Twenty-ninth Sunday of the Year

Scripture Readings (148)

❖ Exod. 17:8–13
❖ Ps. 121:1–2,3–4,5–6,7–8
❖ 2 Tim. 3:14—4:2
❖ Luke 18:1–8

God's Word

A major theme of the Scripture readings is "Persist in faith."

In all three readings today, Moses and the Israelites, Timothy, and the disciples are encouraged to persist in their faith, to not give up when things get tough, and to lean on others in the community when they need help.

When Israel comes under fire from its enemies, Moses is sure that God is on Israel's side. As long as Moses' hands are raised heavenward, Israel prevails. When his arms grow tired, Amalik's forces get the best of the Israelites. What a strange battle plan—outstretched arms instead of weapons. Moses' outstretched arms symbolize all the prayers of the Israelites seeking God's help. We, too, try to reach out to God. But, like Moses, our arms get tired. We get discouraged. We may even give up on prayer and faith for a while. Aaron and Hur are there for Moses when he needs help to keep his arms aloft. We have others in our life to pray for us when we find it difficult to pray.

Today's psalm contains some vivid images of God as protector: a mountain, one who never sleeps, shade from the sun, and a guardian. When we need help, we can turn to God. God is never asleep when we are in need. God protects us from evil as a shade or sunglasses protect us from the sun. As strong as a mountain, God is our guardian against evil. "Our help is from the Lord who made heaven and earth."

Just as Moses had help from others, Timothy is assured in the second reading that he is not alone in keeping the faith. The author encourages this pastor to hold on to faith and traditions. We can learn a lot from friends, family, and the Scriptures to help keep our faith strong. The letter writer places special emphasis on the study of the Scriptures, in which we can find all we need to live a good Christian life.

In this parable, found only in Luke, Jesus tells a story about a widow's persistence, in order to teach about the importance of ongoing prayer. A widow returns again and again to a judge, asking for her case to be considered. The judge has no time for God or man—and certainly not for a widow, one of the poorest of the poor. But after a while, the widow wears the judge down. Maybe the judge only gave the widow what she wanted to get her off his back, but persistence does pay off.

Ordinary Time

If an unjust judge will listen to a widow's plea, just imagine how much more our faithful God will do. Jesus tells all—especially the poor and oppressed—not to lose heart. Persisting in prayer will strengthen our faith. Never give up on prayer.

Jesus closes this teaching with a question we all can ponder: "'When the Son of Man comes, will he find any faith on the earth?'"

Themes for Teens

The following themes from the Scriptures relate to the lives of teens:
- Put your hands in the air for God.
- Never give up.
- God is our guardian.
- God is our guide.
- Keep on praying.

Our Response

Activity

Forty-eight-Hour Prayer-a-thon

This forty-eight-hour prayer-a-thon, keyed to all the readings, involves families and others outside the youth group. It helps teach the young people about the importance of praying together as a community.

Encourage your group of teens to sponsor a forty-eight-hour prayer-a-thon over a weekend. Have the teens make several posters with ninety-six half-hour sign-up spots. Depending on the size of your community, you may want to leave three or four spaces for names in each half-hour slot. You may choose a specific theme for your prayer—such as prayer for peace in our world or prayer for the poor around the world.

As each person signs up, the teens should give him or her a slip of paper to write down the day and time of the pledge and some prayer materials to take home.

Have the teens collect prayer materials for the prayer-a-thon, which might include:
- a book of traditional Catholic prayers
- some Scripture readings related to the chosen theme
- a flyer on the different forms of prayer
- a booklet of prayers the teens have written themselves

You may want to conclude the last hour of the prayer-a-thon with a prayer service or by celebrating the liturgy of the Eucharist as a community.

Activity Ideas

The following activity ideas also relate to the Scripture readings. You may want to read the passage(s) indicated as part of the activity.

- At the start of your gathering, ask the teens to stand up, put their arms straight up over their head, and keep them up as long as they can. When half of the teens have put their arms down, ask them to help the other half to keep their arms aloft. Discuss the following questions:
  - Why was it hard to keep your arms up for a long time?
  - How did help from others make it easier?
  - Why is it difficult to keep praying sometimes?
  - How do we help one another when we pray for one another?

  (Exod. 17:8–13)

- Why not pray to be able to pray? Teach the teens about the beauty and simplicity of a mantra, a prayer of only a few words repeated over and over again, a quiet chant and meditation. As a personal prayer, ask the teens to pray a mantra at home as they fall asleep at night. One example: "Jesus, teach me to pray." Or encourage them to come up with their own mantra. (All readings)

- Introduce this journaling activity in the following way:

  Today's Gospel ends with a question and a challenge. In your journal, answer the following questions:
  - ○ When the Son of Man comes, will he find any faith on the earth?
  - ○ When the Son of Man comes, will he find faith in you?

  (Luke 18:1–8)

- Divide the young people into groups, and allow each group to work on completing a jigsaw puzzle. Direct the teens to think of each piece of their puzzle as a prayer. Say:

  - ○ Why does it take so long to see the finished picture that God has in store for us? As we get older, the puzzle we call our life gets more complicated, our needs become more complicated, and our prayers become more complicated. Just as we need to be persistent and patient to finally complete the puzzle in front of us, so, too, we must persist and persevere in our prayer. (All readings)

Thirtieth Sunday of the Year

Scripture Readings (151)

- ❖ Sir. 35:12–14,16–18
- ❖ Ps. 34:2–3,17–18,19,23
- ❖ 2 Tim. 4:6–8,16–18
- ❖ Luke 18:9–14

God's Word

A major theme of the Scripture readings is "Be humble in prayer."

Last week's readings centered on the importance of persistence in prayer. This week we get instruction on how to pray. We also see again how Jesus places great value on humility as a quality of discipleship.

The first reading assures us that God does not play favorites—God loves us all. Although all who serve God are heard by God, God reserves a special place for the poor and the lonely. We are dependent on God for all things. We are to serve God and to turn to God in prayer. Even when it feels as if we are distant from God, God is close by.

Today's psalm mixes petition and praise, entwining a promise that God will listen with a litany of God's good works. In our society the cries of the poor are drowned out by a sea of materialism and consumerism. Often it appears that no one hears their voice. Yet, above the din, the Lord tunes in first to those who are most in need. They don't need cellular phones or pagers or e-mail to reach God. They have a direct link.

What do you do when everyone turns against you, when you feel abandoned and exhausted from trying to do what is right? Paul, the one in whose name this letter was written, knows what it feels like. But the Lord is not distant, the Lord is right at our side. Paul receives strength from God and is able to go on preaching and teaching. The lion's jaws were a real threat to early Christians; many martyrs lost their life this way. The lions of today wear different disguises but are just as dangerous. Like Paul, we need to fight the good fight and live the good life.

Ordinary Time

In today's Gospel reading, Jesus contrasts the praying styles of two pray-ers, a Pharisee and a tax collector. Pharisees have an elevated place in society, but the tax collectors are looked upon with scorn. This Pharisee uses prayer as a way to catch the public spotlight, feeding his own ego while judging and putting others down. The tax collector approaches God with humility, asking for God's mercy and forgiveness. We are asked to look at the motives behind our prayer. Why do we pray? Is it to bring glory to ourselves or to bring glory and honor to God?

Big egos get in the way of prayer. We need to be genuine when we approach God. It is not who we are or what we do that matters, it's the content of our prayer that is really important. Those who are humble approach God with reverence and respect.

Themes for Teens

The following themes from the Scriptures relate to the lives of teens:
- Pray from the heart.
- God hears us.
- The poor have God's ear.
- Never give up on prayer.
- God is on our side.

Our Response

Activity   How Do We Pray?

This activity asks the young people to think about the motivation for prayer and the right attitude to approach God in prayer.

Write the word *Prayer* on slips of paper, fold them so the word is hidden, and give one to each teen. Ask the teens to look at the word or phrase written on their slip of paper, but not to let anyone else see it.

Instruct the teens to stand in a circle large enough so that they have some room around them to move yet can still see one another. Tell the teens that when you give a signal, they are to strike a pose to describe the word or phrase on their piece of paper. This is sort of a still version of charades. They are to hold the pose until you tell them to sit down. Do not tell the teens that they all have the same word on their paper. On your signal the teens should strike the pose and freeze. Let them look around for a minute before you ask them to sit down.

Ask the teens what prayer looks like. Invite them to volunteer why they depicted prayer the way they did. See if anyone stood still and did not change their pose at all.

Talk about how prayer takes place in many ways and in many settings and cannot be limited to one place or posture. Stress that Jesus is not saying that we should only pray in private. Public prayer in community and by the community is also a blessing.

Activity Ideas

The following activity ideas also relate to the Scripture readings. You may want to read the passage(s) indicated as part of the activity.

- At the end of your meeting, give each of the teens an envelope with a card inside. Tell them not to open the card until right before they go to bed and to read it again after they wake up in the morning. Urge them to take a few minutes to reflect on the card after they read it. The note inside the card should say: "How would your life be different if Jesus stood right by your side all day, every minute of the day?" (2 Tim. 4:6–8,16–18)

- Draw a giant head of a lion on a large piece of poster paper. Make sure the jaws of the lion are wide open. Ask the teens to name some of the traps, temptations, and persecutions we face as Christians today. Write them inside the lion's jaws on the poster. What can we do to avoid the lion's jaws in our daily life? (2 Tim. 4:6–8, 16–18)

- Give each group a piece of poster paper and form small groups. Tell them to write the word *reverence* in big letters across the top. Using the first *R*, ask them to write the word *respect* in large letters going down. With these letters as the base for an acrostic, direct the young people to add words that describe ways we can show reverence and respect for God. (All readings)

- Invite the teens to reflect on the following in their journal: "Imagine you have just finished running a very hard race. You are standing at the finish line of your life. Will you be able to say along with Paul, 'I have fought the good fight, I have finished the race, I have kept the faith'?" (2 Tim. 4:6–8,16–18)

Thirty-first Sunday of the Year

Scripture Readings (154)

- ❖ Wis. 11:22—12:1
- ❖ Ps. 145:1–2,8–9,10–11,13,14
- ❖ 2 Thess. 1:11—2:2
- ❖ Luke 19:1–10

God's Word

A major theme of the Scripture readings is "Seeking out the lost."

The first reading is a wonderful affirmation for each of us and a celebration of God's care for all creation. It echoes the passage from Exodus where God's great strength and compassion brought the Hebrew peoples out of Egypt. Even though we are but a small part of creation—like a drop of dew—we are no less important in God's sight. The author's prayer, "Your imperishable spirit is in all things," challenges us to look at the world through a different lens, with incredible reverence and respect for all God's creation.

The psalmist blesses the name of God again and again. How do we use the name of God? Do we throw it around casually and with little thought? The psalmist promises to praise God every day. What a great goal—to take time every day to praise God.

There are two parts to today's second reading—a prayer that God will complete all good works done in faith, and a warning against false prophets. This reading, like the psalm, reminds us that the best way to praise God's name is to allow God to work through us. The Thessalonians must have been surrounded by false prophets, people who used every trick of the trade to dissuade them from their beliefs. Some said the day of the Lord had already come. The writer urges the Thessalonians to stay true to their faith and to not accept the teachings of those who try to deceive them.

Today's reading from the Gospel of Luke introduces the tax collector Zacchaeus—short in stature, tall in wealth—who is so excited that Jesus is in town that he climbs a tree to get a better look. To Zacchaeus's surprise—and that of the disapproving crowd—Jesus invites himself over to dinner. Zacchaeus, though a social outcast and regarded as a sinner by the Jews, welcomes Jesus with delight.

The story of Zacchaeus assures us that the Spirit of God is indeed with all—with those regarded as sinners, and even with sinners. Zacchaeus seeks salvation by welcoming Jesus into his home, by making amends, and by changing his ways. His encounter with the Lord changes his life. A single encounter with Jesus has the power to change our life, too, and head us in the right direction.

Themes for Teens The following themes from the Scriptures relate to the lives of teens:
- God loves all of creation.
- God's Spirit is in us.
- Praise God forever.
- Listen for God's call.
- Look who is coming to dinner.

Our Response

Activity ## Guess Who Is Coming to Dinner?

This family discussion, keyed to the Gospel reading, is meant to take place at home around the dinner table. It invites families to reflect on the effect Jesus has in their lives and on how to better live as a Christian family.

After sharing today's Scripture readings, give each of the teens a copy of this family discussion activity and urge them to discuss it sometime this week. If the family did not attend Mass together, urge them to reread the Gospel passage before beginning their discussion.

- You and your family are in a crowd waiting to see Jesus and hear him speak. The crowd is standing all around you, so you sit on each other's shoulders in the hope that you will catch a glimpse of Jesus.

  What will your family do when Jesus stops and says to you: "_____ family, hurry down. I mean to stay at your house today."
  - What would you do?
  - How would you react?
  - What would be different about your family dinner conversation with Jesus sitting there?
  - How would a visit from Jesus change your family?

Activity Ideas The following activity ideas also relate to the Scripture readings. You may want to read the passage(s) indicated as part of the activity.

- In the first reading, we learn that God's Spirit is in all things. In small groups, discuss the following questions:
  - If God is in all things, how should it make a difference in the way we treat other people?
  - How should it make a difference in the way we treat the gifts God has given us?
  - How can we do a better job of taking care of the gifts of nature?

    You may want to talk briefly about ways the teens can recycle at home, at school, and in the parish. (Wis. 11:22—12:1)

- In their journal, ask the teens to write on the following topic: "At the end of a busy school day, reflect on what you did, who you talked with, what you saw and heard. Recall what you saw, heard, smelled, touched, and tasted that made you aware of Jesus in your life today . . .
  - in the people you met
  - in the places you went
  - in the things you saw
  - in the words you heard
  - in the gifts of nature
  - in yourself"

(All readings)

- Zacchaeus was not searching for Jesus, but Jesus found him. It is true that Jesus will find us where we are, but we also need to search for Jesus. Invite the teens to participate in a scavenger hunt. The goal is to find Jesus. You can do this activity right at your meeting site or between meetings. Following are some samples of scavenger hunt requests:
  - Find someone who has received the sacrament of confirmation.
  - Find an example of a good Samaritan in today's newspaper.
  - Find something with the words to a traditional Catholic prayer written on it.
  - Find a Bible and turn to today's Gospel reading.
  - Find an example of Jesus in nature, but leave it where you found it.
  - Find a can of food to give to the food bank.
  - Find a message from Jesus in a song currently playing on the radio.

  (Luke 19:1–10)

- The psalm proclaims: "I will praise your name for ever, my king and my God." Ask the teens to brainstorm a list of the many different names we use for God. Use one of the names to replace each reference to God in the first reading. Invite one young person to proclaim the first reading, pausing after each line so the entire group can respond, "Amen!" (Wis. 11:22—12:1; Ps. 145:1–2,8–9,10–11,13,14)

Thirty-second Sunday of the Year

Scripture Readings (157)

- ❖ 2 Macc. 7:1–2,9–14
- ❖ Ps. 17:1,5–6,8,15
- ❖ 2 Thess. 2:16—3:5
- ❖ Luke 20:27–38

God's Word

A major theme of the Scripture readings is "Life after death."

The first reading recounts the story of seven brothers and their mother who choose death rather than deny their faith. In this case they were forced to eat pork, strictly forbidden by the Jewish faith. One after another they show their courage to their enemies. They curse their tormentors, yet profess faith in God and unflagging hope in the promise of resurrection. This excerpt was written when the Jews were being persecuted by Seleucid kings. It was retold to give people hope that the just are rewarded by life after death.

The psalmist finds real joy in the glory of the Lord. The writer asks God to take care of him as the "apple of your eye" and to find him shelter in the "shadow of your wings." God is always there for us when we are in need.

The second reading is from one of two letters giving us a glimpse of the early church in Thessalonia and its struggles. The writer asks the Thessalonians to be persistent in their struggle, to work only for the Gospel, and to pray for one another. The Thessalonians must pray for strength and courage to continue proclaiming the word of God. Prayer is highlighted here as a powerful force in the believing community. The reading begins and ends with a blessing of hope and a consolation that the Lord will rule all of our hearts.

Ordinary Time

In today's Gospel reading, a group of Sadducees—a priestly aristocratic group—pose a hypothetical question to Jesus in the hope of tripping him up. The Sadducees do not believe in the resurrection of the body, and they object to Jesus' teaching on the subject. Belief in the resurrection of the body is a key part of the Christian faith. The Sadducees cannot find anything written about it in Jewish Law, so they refuse to listen. Once again, the observance of the Law comes in conflict with the teaching of Jesus. Jesus is not going to get caught up in their debate about who was married to whom. Jesus uses the Scriptures to get out of the Sadducees' trap. Jesus says that life after death is very different from the life we live now. Nothing can end our relationship with God—not even death.

Themes for Teens

The following themes from the Scriptures relate to the lives of teens:
- God will raise us up.
- There is life after death.
- Prayer draws us together.
- Hope in the Resurrection.
- God is there for us.

Our Response

Activity   A Tree of Life

This prayer experience is keyed to the readings as a whole. It gives the young people an opportunity to remember friends and family members who have died, and it reinforces the message of life after death found in today's readings.
- *Preparation.* Place a large, dead tree branch in the center of your prayer space. Give each teen a long, thin strip of white paper. Ask the teens to write the name of a relative or friend who has died on the paper. Copy the names onto a single sheet for the person who will be reading the litany of our saints.
- *Call to prayer.* Sing the opening song, "By Name I Have Called You," by Carey Landry (*Glory and Praise,* vol. 1 [Phoenix, AZ: North American Liturgy Resources, 1990], pages 84–85). Ask the teens to come forward one at a time and fasten the name of their loved one around a branch of the tree.
- *Litany of the saints.* This can be found in a book of common prayers.
- *Storytelling.* Invite the teens to share a memory of a loved one who has died. This part of the prayer should be optional. Do not require any young person to speak.
- *Litany of our saints.* Pray as in the litany of the saints above, inserting names of the teens' deceased loved ones.
- *Tree of life.* Invite the teens to come forward and place white carnations on the tree by the spot where they placed the name of their loved one. Play quiet instrumental music in the background.

Activity Ideas

The following activity ideas also relate to the Scripture readings. You may want to read the passage(s) indicated as part of the activity.

- Watch the movie *Defending Your Life,* starring Meryl Streep. Afterward, ask the teens to describe how heaven is portrayed in the movie.
  - ○ What do you think heaven will be like?
  - ○ What do you hope heaven will be like?
  - ○ After reading today's readings, what do the Scriptures tell us that we have to look forward to?

(All readings)

- After sharing today's second reading, share some blessings from the Catholic *Book of Blessings*, by the International Commission on English in the Liturgy, or some ethnic blessings, such as the "Irish Blessing." Ask the teens if they have ever had a new house blessed or if their family has taken an Easter basket to church to have the food blessed on Holy Saturday. Ask them to give examples of blessings they have received. Remind them that blessings are not just for things but for people, too, and that we are blessings for one another. Close by asking the teens to write blessings for the other teens in their group. (2 Thess. 2:16—3:5)

- Invite a parish priest to talk to the young people about the funeral liturgy and why it is now called the Mass of the Resurrection, and about why priests wear white vestments to symbolize life after death. If a priest is not available, you may want to walk the teens through a funeral liturgy found in the *Sacramentary*. The young people can identify wording and symbols that profess the Catholic belief in life after death. (2 Macc. 7:1–2,9–14; Luke 20:27–38)

- Give each teen a piece of gray construction paper or cardboard shaped like a tombstone. Give them some quiet time to write their own epitaph. Ask them: "How do you want to be remembered? How does this affect the way you live your life right now?" (All readings)

Thirty-third Sunday of the Year

Scripture Readings (160)
- ❖ Mal. 3:19–20
- ❖ Ps. 98:5–6,7–8,9
- ❖ 2 Thess. 3:7–12
- ❖ Luke 21:5–19

God's Word

A major theme of the Scripture readings is "Judgment day."

All of the readings today tell us that we cannot sit around waiting for judgment day to come; we need to keep working for the Kingdom.

The first reading describes a judgment by fire for all those who have no need for God and for those who do evil. Sometimes we think that only those who purposely commit evil will be left out of the Kingdom. Those who care little for God face the same fate. Yet those who approach God with reverence and respect and who act with justice in their everyday life are healed by the sun of justice, whom Christians interpret to be Jesus Christ.

The psalm picks up on the theme of justice. God is portrayed as ruler and sovereign over all the earth, and justice is the hallmark of God's Reign. The psalmist urges all to praise God with an orchestra of harps, trumpets, and horns.

According to the second reading, the Thessalonians are getting a little out of hand. Because they believe that Jesus will return with the judgment of God soon, some of the folks are a bit lazy, others sit around gossiping all day, and some are a bit unruly. The author has a very different perspective on how to wait for the return of the Lord. He tells them to get to work, to stop mooching off of others, and to carry out their responsibilities. The author tells them to look to him as an example.

Today's Gospel reading is really frightening. It continues what we read in Malachi about the end of all things as we know them—the end of the world. Jesus describes a tough time of suffering before the end of the world—wars, famine, earthquakes, and other natural disasters. Jesus also speaks of the personal persecution we will face in the name of our faith. Our family and friends will turn against us and we may even die—all because we are followers of Jesus. Yet, as we read in Malachi, those who follow the Lord will be protected. We are not alone in our times of trial. God guides and protects us.

Themes for Teens

The following themes from the Scriptures relate to the lives of teens:
- The end is coming.
- God is justice.
- Don't sit around; work for God.
- Christians can't be lazy.
- God saves us from evil.

Our Response

Activity   Fire and Light

This icebreaker is keyed to the first reading. It uses the qualities of fire and light to help the young people describe something about themselves. The scriptural study invites the teens to explore the rich symbolism of fire and light in the Hebrew Scriptures and the Christian Testament.

- *Reflection.* Teach the teens how to build a campfire or a fire in a fireplace. Ask them to watch and listen quietly so that they can hear and see the fire grow from a spark to a flame.
- *Icebreaker.* After the fire is burning, direct the teens to use a quality of light to describe something about themselves. You can give some examples:
  - I am like a tiny flame . . .
  - I am like a flicker of fire . . .
  - I am like a crackling fire . . .
  - I am like a glowing ember . . .
  - I am like a warm glow . . .
  - I am like a blazing fire . . .
  - I am like a roaring blaze . . .
- *Scriptural study.* Break into small groups—still remaining around the campfire or fireplace—and find examples of the ways fire and light play a key role in the tradition of both the Hebrew Scriptures and the Christian Testament. Then ask a spokesperson from each group to share at least one example from the Scriptures and what it taught him or her about God.

Activity Ideas

The following activity ideas also relate to the Scripture readings. You may want to read the passage(s) indicated as part of the activity.

- Divide the teens into pairs and tell them to face each other. Ask one person in the pair to imitate everything the other person does for 3 minutes. Have them switch roles and repeat the activity. Use the following questions for discussion:
  - Would you behave differently day-to-day if you knew a younger child was imitating everything you do?
  - Who are some of the people you imitate?
  - What do you try to imitate about them?

    In the second reading, Paul asks the Thessalonians to imitate him. How can we imitate Jesus to live as better Christians? (2 Thess. 3:7–12)

- We struggle against the forces of evil even today, just as those living in Malachi's time and the time of the early Christians did. Discuss the following questions:
  - What are some of the sufferings you have endured in your life?
  - Are you afraid to take a stand—against abortion, drugs, and the like—because your "friends" will turn against you?
  - Do your friends ever shun you or put you down because you are a Catholic?

    (Mal. 3:19–20; Luke 21:5–19)

- Today's psalm urges us to praise God with harp, trumpet, horn, and song. Visit a first- or second-grade religious education class and help the children make instruments for a "Praise Band." The teens can help the children put rice between two paper plates or a few pennies in orange juice cans to make shakers, decorate paper towel tubes for horns, and decorate large oatmeal containers for drums. Then they can teach the children a song to sing while playing their instruments. (Ps. 98:5–6,7–8,9)

- Reread the passage from Thessalonians, and tell the teens to answer the following questions in their journal:
  - Do you work hard, or are you a busybody, always busy but never accomplishing much?
  - What are some areas of your life where you need to work harder?
  - What can you do to stop gossiping or meddling in other people's business?

    (2 Thess. 3:7–12)

Thirty-fourth Sunday of the Year (Christ the King)

Scripture Readings (163)

- ❖ 2 Sam. 5:1–3
- ❖ Ps. 122:1–2,3–4,4–5
- ❖ Col. 1:12–20
- ❖ Luke 23:35–43

God's Word A major theme of the Scripture readings is "Ruling from the cross."

Throughout the Hebrew Scriptures and the Christian Testament, we call God by many names. All of today's readings call on us to worship God as King.

In the first reading, David takes over as king of Israel. Saul has died and David takes his place. The tribes of Israel come to pay their respects, but it is the mandate of the Lord that really counts. David is a symbol of God's authority. God reaches out to the people through David. The king must be much more than a ruler of the people. David must be a shepherd, guiding the flock.

Today's psalm is a psalm of pilgrimage, perhaps prayer, as the people of Israel walk to the holy city of Jerusalem. Pilgrimages are often walking events where people travel for days and even weeks to a special holy place to offer praise and thanksgiving to God and to ask for many blessings. We, too, walk

Ordinary Time

with the Chosen People of Israel. We may not walk as far, but we must make time in our busy life to praise and thank our God.

The second reading is a hymn in praise of the greatness of Christ. Through the blood of the cross, Jesus forgives our sins and brings us into the Kingdom. Jesus is both earthly king and divine king, the center of all creation and the head of the body, which is the church. Jesus sheds his blood so that we may be redeemed.

The Gospel reading is an excerpt from Luke's story of the Crucifixion, in which an innocent Jesus is put to death. What a strange way to treat a king. Instead of sitting on a throne, Jesus is nailed to a cross. Jesus' crown is not made of gold, but of thorns. Instead of the best food and wine, Jesus gets sour vinegar. Instead of glory, Jesus receives only jeers. Jesus is indeed a king like no other. Yet in Jesus' suffering, he won for us the Kingdom of God.

The sign above Jesus' head read "King of the Jews" and was placed there to mock Jesus. The two criminals crucified with Jesus react differently. One scoffs at Jesus. The other fears God. Jesus—in all his pain—reaches out to the repentant criminal and promises him a place in heaven. This king rules with love, not armies. Jesus' power is revealed on the cross.

Themes for Teens The following themes from the Scriptures relate to the lives of teens:
- Jesus is the Shepherd King.
- Walk the walk of God.
- Jesus redeems us.
- Jesus is a king like no other.
- He rules from the cross.
- Jesus' innocent suffering is an act of love.

Our Response

Activity **A King Like No Other**

This activity is keyed to the readings as a whole. It invites the young people to contrast earthly kings with Christ our King. It also gives them an opportunity to make a cross and to continue the Catholic tradition of hanging a sign of Jesus in their room at home.
- *Discussion.* Draw a big outline of a crown on one piece of poster board and an outline of a cross on another. Ask the teens to write adjectives on the crown to describe a king. On the cross, ask the teens to write words to describe Jesus. How are the words different? How are they the same? What do we learn about Christ our King in today's scriptural readings?
- *Craft.* Ask the teens to cut a cross—roughly 6-by-8 inches—out of heavy white paper. Using gold yarn to symbolize Jesus' kingship, have them outline the cross and continue using the yarn to fill in the center of the cross until it is completely filled. Urge the teens to take the cross home and hang it in their room.

Activity Ideas The following activity ideas also relate to the Scripture readings. You may want to read the passage(s) indicated as part of the activity.

- Make King Cake, a Mardi Gras tradition from New Orleans. Hide a small crown in the cake batter before baking. Serve each teen a piece of the cake. Provide the person who finds the crown with a small "cross in my pocket" memento to give to each teen to remember Christ the King Sunday. (All readings)

- Before your meeting, ask each of the teens to bring a crucifix from home. If some teens don't have one, they can bring a picture with them. Compare the different images of Jesus on the cross, especially contrasting the ones of gold and jewels with those made simply of wood. Then ask the following questions:
  - Why is the symbol of our King a cross rather than a crown?
  - What does a crown symbolize?
  - What does a cross symbolize?

(All readings)

- Direct the teens to go home and look for a cross hanging somewhere in their own house or in the house of a relative. Let the teens interview their relatives and ask them why they hang a cross in their house and what it means to them. The next time you gather as a group, invite the teens to share some of these family traditions. (Luke 23:35–43)

- In their journal, ask the teens to draw the outline of a banner or a sign. Urge them to reflect on this question: "In today's Gospel, we hear that the sign above Jesus' head read 'King of the Jews.' If you could replace that sign, what would you write?" (Luke 23:35–43)

- Ask the teens about experiences they have had or know about in which innocent people have suffered because of love. (Luke 23:35–43)

Audiovisual Distributor

Billy Budd Films
235 East Fifty-seventh Street
New York, NY 10022
212-755-3968

Resources

Faley, Roland J. *Footprints on the Mountain: Preaching and Teaching the Sunday Readings*. Mahwah, NJ: Paulist Press, 1994.

Hamma, Robert M. "The Lectionary: Heart of the Bible." *Catholic Update* (St. Anthony Messenger Press, Cincinnati, OH), C1090, 1990.

_____, ed. *A Catechumen's Lectionary*. Mahwah, NJ: Paulist Press, 1988.

Harris, Maria. *Fashion Me a People: Curriculum in the Church*. Louisville, KY: Westminster/John Knox Press, 1989.

Homily Service: An Ecumenical Resource for Sharing the Word. Cycle C, vol. 26, nos. 9–12, and vol. 27, nos. 1–8, 1993–94. Available from the Liturgical Conference, 8750 Georgia Avenue, Suite 123, Silver Spring, MD 20910-3621.

National Federation for Catholic Youth Ministry (NFCYM). *The Challenge of Adolescent Catechesis: Maturing in Faith*. Washington, DC: NFCYM, 1986.

_____. *The Challenge of Catholic Youth Evangelization: Called to Be Witnesses and Storytellers*. New Rochelle, NY: Don Bosco Multimedia, 1993.

Pontifical Bible Commission. "The Interpretation of the Bible in the Church." *Origins* 23, no. 29, 6 January 1994.

Sanchez, Patricia Datchuck. *The Word We Celebrate: Commentary on the Sunday Lectionary, Years A, B, and C*. Kansas City, MO: Sheed and Ward, 1989.

Smith, Virginia. "If I Can Find My Bible, What Do I Do Next?" *Youth Update* (St. Anthony Messenger Press), December 1990.

United States Catholic Conference (USCC). *The Bible in Catechesis, The Living Light*. Washington, DC: Department of Education, USCC, n.d.

Index of Themes

Index of Gospel Readings

Acknowledgments (*continued*)

The scriptural quotations marked NRSV are from the New Revised Standard Version of the Bible, copyright © 1989 by the Division of Christian Education of the National Council of the Churches of Christ in the United States of America. All rights reserved.

All other scriptural quotations are from the New American Bible. Copyright © 1970 by the Confraternity of Christian Doctrine, 3211 Fourth Street NE, Washington, DC 20017. All rights reserved.

The excerpt on page 7 is from *The Challenge of Catholic Youth Evangelization: Called to Be Witnesses and Storytellers,* by the National Federation for Catholic Youth Ministry (NFCYM) (New Rochelle, NY: Don Bosco Multimedia, 1993), pages 5–6. Copyright © 1993 by the NFCYM.

The keys to Scripture study on page 11 are from *Fashion Me a People: Curriculum in the Church,* by Maria Harris (Louisville, KY: Westminster/John Knox Press, 1989), pages 60–61. Copyright © 1989 by Westminster/John Knox Press.

The story on page 16 is adapted from "God Gives Us Fresh Clay," by Barbara Gargiulo, in *Religion Teacher's Journal,* September 1996, page 19.

The prayer on page 26 is from *Advent Prayers for Families: Every-Day Virtues,* by Gwen Costello (Mystic, CT: Twenty-Third Publications, n.d.), n.p.

The list of proverbs on page 28 is from "Beginning-of-the-Year Wisdom," by Melannie Svoboda, SND, in *Religion Teacher's Journal,* September 1996, page 13.

The drawing on page 30 is from *Wind and Fire,* December 1996, vol. 3, no. 4, a newsletter published by the Holy Spirit Parish, Viriginia Beach, VA.

The activity describing a Seder plate on page 45 is adapted from *The Jewish Holiday Cookbook,* by Gloria Kaufer Greene (New York: Times Books, Random House, 1985), pages 238–239. Copyright © 1985 by Gloria Kaufer Greene.

The poem on pages 54–55, "Easter Eggs for Jesus" by Jeff Martinson, is taken from *Parish Teacher,* March 1996, vol. 19, no. 7, page 14.

The self-inventory on violence on page 65 is adapted from "Making a Stand Against Violence," by Tom Everson, in *Youth Update,* August 1995, n.p.

The Yarn Web Prayer on page 67 by Monica Brown is adapted from *Hard Times Catalog for Youth Ministry* (Loveland, CO: Group Books, 1982), page 212. Copyright © 1982 by Marilyn and Dennis Benson.

The hospitality test on page 104 is from "Impressions: Ten Reasons New Kids Will/Won't Come Back to Your Youth Group," by Stephanie Caro, in *Group,* September–October 1996, page 45.

The prayer service on pages 106–107 is from *Teaching Manual for PrayerWays,* by Maryann Hakowski (Winona, MN: Saint Mary's Press, 1995), pages 44–46 and handout 4–A. Copyright © 1995 by Saint Mary's Press. All rights reserved.

The story of "The Prodigal Daughter" by Lisa-Marie Calderone-Stewart on pages 121–122 is from *Faith Works for Junior High* (Winona, MN: Saint Mary's Press, 1993), pages 70–71. Copyright © 1993 by Saint Mary's Press. All rights reserved.